A Chronological and Comparative Study of
Body Language in English
and American Literature

Studies in the History of the English Language **8**

A Chronological and Comparative Study of Body Language in English and American Literature

Edited by
Masahiro Hori, Yuko Ikeda
& Keisuke Koguchi

The Japanese Association for
Studies in the History of the English Language

Kaitakusha

First published 2018

ISBN978-4-7589-2268-5 C3382

© The several authors 2018

All rights reserved; no part of this publication may be reproduced, stored in a retrieval system, or transmitted in any form without written permission from the publisher.

Kaitakusha Publishing Co., Ltd.

1-5-2 Mukogaoka, Bunkyo Ward, Tokyo 113-0023, JAPAN

Contents

Editors and Contributors   vii

Preface   xi
   Masahiro Hori

To raise one's eyes in Old and Middle English   1
   Takuto Watanabe

The Use of 'Hand(s)' in Shakespeare's Romance Plays   23
   Noritaka Tomimura

From Convention to Creation: Blushing in Jane Austen
with Reference to her Predecessors   41
   Yuko Ikeda

The Characters' Eyes and Eye Behavior in Gaskell's *Sylvia's Lovers*   63
   Aiko Saiki

Body Language in Dickens's *Hard Times*: The Characters' Eyes
and Eye Behavior   85

    Masahiro Hori

Body Language in Dickens with Special Reference to 'Hand'   109

    Keisuke Koguchi

Facial Expressions and Eye Behavior in American Literature:
A Case Study of Ernest Hemingway's *The Sun Also Rises*   133

    Hirotoshi Takeshita

Index   165

Editors and Contributors

Masahiro HORI, Kumamoto Gakuen University. Major publications: *Investigating Dickens' style: A collocational analysis* (Basingstoke: Palgrave Macmillan, 2004); *Introduction to collocation studies in English* (in Japanese); Masahiro Hori & Ichiro Akano (general editors), *English Corpus Studies Series* (7 Volumes) (in Japanese) (Tokyo: Hituzi Shobo, 2015–18).

Yuko IKEDA, Kumamoto University (part-time lecturer). Major publications: 'From "liveliness" to "tranquillity": A lexical approach to Jane Austen's *Pride and Prejudice* and *Mansfield Park*,' in Masahiro Hori, et al. (eds.), *Stylistic studies of literature: In honour of Professor Hiroyuki Ito* (Bern: Peter Lang, 2009); 'The development of playful mind: Samuel Richardson's *Grandison* and Jane Austen's *Pride and Prejudice*,' *Kumamoto Studies in English Language and Literature* 53 (2010); 'Comedy and femininity: Reading *Evelina*' (in Japanese) in The Jane Austen Society of Japan (ed.), *New insights into Jane Austen and her contemporaries* (Tokyo: Sairyusha, 2017).

Keisuke KOGUCHI, Yasuda Women's University. Major publications: *Repetition in Dickens's* A Tale of Two Cities*: An exploration into his linguistic artistry* (Hiroshima: Keisuisha, 2009); Sadao Ando (ed.), *The CROWN dictionary of English phrases* (in Japanese) (Tokyo: Sanseido, 2014); 'Stylistic use of personal pronouns in *A Tale of Two Cities*' in Ken Nakagawa (editor in chief), *Studies in Modern English: The Thirtieth Anniversary Publication of the Modern English Association* (Tokyo: Eihosha, 2014).

viii

Aiko SAIKI, Kumamoto University (part-time lecturer). Major publications: 'The role of money in *Silas Marner*,' *Kumamoto Studies in English Language and Literature* 51 (2008); 'Eyes in *Sylvia's Lovers*' (in Japanese) in The Gaskell Society of Japan (ed.), *Elizabeth Gaskell and the tradition of English literature: On the bicentennial commemoration of her birth* (Osaka: Osaka Kyoiku Tosho, 2010); 'The use of imagery in "Crooked Branch"' (in Japanese) in The Gaskell Society of Japan (ed.), *A study of the shorter fiction of Elizabeth Gaskell: On the sesquicentennial commemoration of her death* (Osaka: Osaka Kyoiku Tosho, 2015).

Hirotoshi TAKESHITA, Shokei University. Major publications: 'Some syntactic and stylistic observations on absolutes in *Adventures of Huckleberry Finn*,' in Masahiro Hori et al. (eds.), *Stylistic studies of literature: In honour of Professor Hiroyuki Ito* (Bern: Peter Lang, 2009); 'Some stylistic aspects of Ernest Hemingway's "The Undefeated"' (in Japanese), *English Usage and Style* 28 (2011); 'Collocational study of Mark Twain's novels made with electric corpora: With special reference to body-part nouns for facial expressions in *The Prince and the Pauper*' (in Japanese), in Masahiro Hori (ed.), *The Hituzi Companion to English Corpus Studies: Corpus and English Stylistics* (Tokyo: Hituzi Shobo, 2016).

Noritaka TOMIMURA, the National Institute of Technology, Kure College, Japan. Major publications: 'Shakespeare's use of song' in Masahiro Hori, et al. (eds.), *Stylistic studies of literature: In honour of Professor Hiroyuki Ito* (Bern: Peter Lang, 2009); 'The use of music in Shakespeare's plays in comparison with the plays of Kyd and Marlowe' (in Japanese) in *Studies of Shakespeare's works: Plays, poems and music* (Tokyo: Eihosha, 2016); 'Improving project implementation abilities through the production of short movies' (in Japanese), *Journal of Japanese society for engineering education* 66-1 (2018).

Takuto, WATANABE, Kumamoto Gakuen University. Major publications: 'On the development of the immediate future use of *be about to* in the history of English with special reference to Late Modern English,' *English Linguistics* 28 (2011); 'On the transition from *ymb* to *about* in Old and Middle English,' in Michio Hosaka et al. (eds.) *Phases of the history of English* (Frankfurt am Main: Peter Lang, 2013); 'Changes in future expressions in Modern English Bibles' (in Japanese), *Studies in Modern English* 32 (2016).

Preface

This collection of seven essays covering a wide range of historical periods from Old English to the twentieth century, is the eighth volume in the series Studies in the History of the English Language. It is the first product of a research project on the history of English expression in literature as a new perspective in historical stylistics. As a first step in this project we have focused our attention on a chronological and comparative study of body language in English and American literature. Our aim is to contribute toward the establishment of a whole system and functions of body language in the history of English expression in literature.

Body language, as an essential part of non-verbal communication, is an important and possibly indispensable component in everyday communication. In real life, for example, upon receiving some delightful news, it is common to say that joy is written on the face. A heart overcome with deep grief is accompanied with tears of sorrow and a pained expression. Similarly, literature often attempts to describe such non-verbal behavior. For instance, in *Little Dorrit*, Dickens writes 'Arthur's increasing wish to speak of something very different was by this time *so plainly written on his face*, that Flora stopped in *a tender look*, and asked him what it was?' (Book II, Chapter 9) while in *Bleak House* he writes 'Phil *intimates by sidling back a pace or two, with a very unaccountable wrench of his wry face*, that he does not regard the transaction as being made more promising by this incident' (Chapter 34). These are just two examples of the range of expressions that play an important role in these two texts.

The manner in which body language is employed, including descriptions of gesture, posture, and of such body parts as face and hand, represents a significant aspect in many literary works. Even eye behavior and eye contact between characters, as examined in detail in two papers in this collection, may also function as important carriers of meaning, especially as emotional displays and emblems of the relationships between characters. These expressions, however, have not been fully discussed in the academic field of stylistics, much less in historical stylistics.

Within the academic study of body language in literature, Barbara Korte's *Body Language in Literature* (1997) has served as a bible for all the contributors in this collection. Her work not only established a general theory and a critical framework elucidating the varieties of body language found in literary discourse, but also presented abundant evidence and materials from eighty novels on the functions and historical developments of body language in literature. Consulting her book, all of us have analyzed the literary texts with close attention to particular body parts such as eye, hand and facial expressions, attempting not merely to ascertain the truth and usefulness of her theory and framework but to break new ground and to create new possibilities in the study of body language in historical stylistics in literature as well.

In concluding this preface, on behalf of the contributors to this book, I wish to express our academic indebtedness to Hiroyuki Ito, Professor Emeritus at Kumamoto University, who passed away in July 2017. We would like to dedicate this volume to his memory.

This work was supported by JSPS KAKENHI Grant Number 16K02788.

Masahiro Hori
Kumamoto Gakuen University
Autumn 2018

To raise one's eyes in Old and Middle English[1]

Takuto Watanabe

1. Introduction

To raise one's eyes is a relatively common collocation in English today and is often employed as a literary device to express something beyond the literal sense. In terms of the popularity of the collocation, *raised* is the ninth most frequent lexical verb among those occurring within three words that precede *eyes* in the BNC (Table 1). This might appear noteworthy because, while the verbs in the list largely refer to eyelid movement, such as *open* or *close*, the verb *raise* describes the gaze directed upwards. Regarding the context of usage, *to raise one's eyes* is distributed almost exclusively in imaginative texts in the BNC (Table 2), and is employed to describe a person's internal feelings or the act of praying to God, as in the following quotations:[2]

(1) a. 'What did happen to us in Seville, Fernando?' She *raised her eyes* to look into his. Perhaps now she might get an idea of what went wrong. His eyes were unreadable but . . . . (BNC: JY4)
   b. Charsky leaned back against the pillows and *raised his eyes* to the ceiling as if thanking the Almighty. (BNC: AE0)

---

[1] I would like to express my gratitude to Professor Akiyuki Jimura and Professor Masahiro Hori for their comments and suggestions, and to Christie Provenzano for stylistic improvements.
[2] Italics in example sentences are mine.

In (1a), the woman's raising her eyes expresses her anxiety to know the man's point of view about the situation. In (1b), *raised his eyes* is understandable not only in the literal sense (i.e. his face is turned upwards) but also in the religious sense (i.e. his eyes are directed to heaven, where God exists). These instances suggest that when this gesture is described, the purpose is usually to express something more than its literal meaning. This paper, by exploring its usage in Old and Middle English texts, shows that the expression goes back to biblical contexts and was eventually adopted into English literature. In addition, it shows that the modern function of the gesture as a literary device seems to have its roots in later Middle English, as evidenced by Chaucer's usage of it.

The rest of the paper is organised as follows. Sections 2 and 3 present data from the Old and Middle English periods, respectively. Based on the data, Section 4 discusses the history of the expression in detail. Section 5 offers some conclusions regarding this subject.

Table 1. Lexical verbs occurring within three words before *eyes* in the BNC

Rank	Verb	Freq.	Rank	Verb	Freq.
1	*closed*	759	6	*open*	131
2	*opened*	465	7	*met*	129
3	*close*	224	8	*kept*	122
4	*shut*	190	9	*raised*	115
5	*keep*	153	10	*narrowed*	109

Table 2. Genre distribution of *raised . . . eyes* (with up to two intervening words) in the BNC

Genre	per mil	%
Educational	0.54	7.6
Imaginative	6.12	86.1
Leisure	0.29	4.1
Social Science	0.06	0.8
World Affairs	0.1	1.4

2. Old English

The data for the Old English period was retrieved by searching the *Dictionary of Old English Corpus* (Healey 2000) for *eagan* (the accusative plural form of *eage* 'eye').[3] Then, sentences containing a verb with the meaning 'to raise' were manually collected.

One thing that should be noted about the history of *to raise one's eyes* is that different verbs are used in different time periods. In Old English, the verb that closely collocates with *eagan* is *hebban* 'to heave' (including the prefixed forms *ahebban*, *upahebban*, and *uphebban*). The only exception is the usage of *abregdan* 'to raise' in two texts of Benedict's *Rules* to translate Ps. 131:1 as in (2a–b), which is, in light of the prevalence of *hebban,* likely to be a variant of *upahebban* as in (2c):[4]

(2) a. Drihten, nis min heorte onhafen, ne *mine eagan up abrodene* (BenR 7.22.13)

    b. Drihten, nis min heorte onhefð, ne *myne eagen up abrodene*; (BenRW 7.31.10)

    c. la drihten nis upahafen heorte mine nana *upahafen* sind *eagan mine.* (BenRGl 7.27.6)

    'LORD, my heart is not proud, nor are my eyes haughty;' (Ps. 131:1)

As we will see in Section 3, *hebban* continues to be the only verb that has a strong tie with *eagan* until the beginning of the Middle English period.

---

[3] The search was made with AntConc (3.4.4) using regular expressions '¥bæa*g[aeou]{0,2}n¥b' and '¥b[ae]+g[aeou]{0,2}n¥b.'

[4] Citation sources in Section 2 refer to the *Dictionary of Old English* short titles. Throughout this paper, biblical quotations in Present-day English are taken from the Revised English Bible.

4

Table 3. *To raise one's eyes* in Old English biblical translations and quotations[5]

Book and verse	Freq.[6]	Text
Gen. 13:10	1	*The Old English Version of the Heptateuch*
Ps. 120:1 (121:1)	11	*Psalms*
Ps. 122:1 (123:1)	11	*Psalms*
Ps. 131:1	3	Benedict's *Rule*
Dan. 4:3	1	*Catholic Homilies*
Matt. 17:8	1	*The Anglo-Saxon Gospels*
Luke 16:23	2	*The Anglo-Saxon Gospels*, Gregory's *Dialogues*
Luke 18:13	6	*The Anglo-Saxon Gospels, Catholic Homilies,* Benedict's *Rule*
John 4:35	1	*The Anglo-Saxon Gospels*
John 6:5	2	*The Anglo-Saxon Gospels, Catholic Homilies*
John 11:41	1	*The Anglo-Saxon Gospels*
John 17:1	1	*The Anglo-Saxon Gospels*

Table 4. *To raise one's eyes* in Old English religious texts other than biblical translations or quotations

Text	Freq.[7]	Text	Freq.
Ælfric's *Lives of Saints*	3	*Holy Rood*	1
Bede's *Ecclesiastical History*	4	*Life of Guthlac*	1
Blickling Homiliies	1	*Martyrology*	2
Gregory's *Dialogues*	2 (3)	*Nativity of Mary the Virgin*	1 (2)

---

[5] 'Biblical quotations' are passages cited from the Bible (cf. Cook 1903).
[6] The figures indicate the total number of occurrences of the same verse in different texts or manuscripts.
[7] The figures in brackets indicate the total number of occurrences of the same passage in different manuscripts. The same applies to Table 5.

As shown in Tables 3 and 4, *to raise one's eyes* is distributed exclusively in religious texts and no instance was found in non-religious texts. The most common context is where one in prayer raises his/her eyes to God or heaven. (3a–b) are translations of biblical verses, and such instances account for eight of the thirteen verses in Table 3.

(3) a. *Hof* ic *mine eagan* to þam hean beorge, þær ic fultum fand fælne æt þearfe. (PPs 120.1)

'IF I lift up my eyes to the hills, where shall I find help?' (Ps. 121:1)

  b. Ða stod se manfulla feorran & nolde furðun *his eagan ahebban* up to þam heofone, (Lk (WSCp) 18.13)

'But the other [the tax-collector] kept his distance and would not even raise his eyes to heaven,' (Luke 18:13)

As is clear from the context, the gesture of raising eyes is connected with prayer in the instances above. In (3a), the psalmist raises his eyes to the hills seeking for help, but it is not that he looks up at the hills around him; rather, he raises his eyes to God as we read in Ps. 123:1 'I LIFT my eyes to you whose throne is in heaven.' On the contrary, in (3b), the tax-collector (*se manfulla* 'the evil one') dares not raise his eyes because of his qualms of conscience, even though he is in the temple to pray.

In contexts other than biblical translations and quotations, too, the gesture is frequently related to the scene of prayer (ten of the fifteen instances listed in Table 4), as in (4a–b) below:

(4) a. Þa *ahof* se halga to heofonum *his eagan*, his Drihten biddende and bealdlice cweðende, (ÆLS (George) 108)

'Then the saint raised his eyes to heaven, praying to his Lord and boldly saying,'

  b. And ða Sanctus Albanus . . . eode ða to þære burnan þe ic ær sæde, & *his eagan ahof* upp to heofonum, þa sona adrugode se stream & beah for his fotum, swa þæt he mihte dryge ofergangan. (Bede 1 7.38.13)

'And when St. Albanus went to the river I mentioned before and raised his eyes to heaven, then the stream immediately dried up and gave way to him so that he could walk over the dry ground.'

(4a) is a straightforward usage of *to raise one's eyes* in the scene of prayer. In (4b), St. Albanus' raising his eyes to heaven appears to function as a symbolic gesture indicating that the ability to perform a miracle comes from God. This description might be comparable to, for example, Jesus' looking up to heaven when he fed five thousand people with five loaves and two fishes (Matt. 14:19).

The remaining instances in Tables 3 and 4 include those that refer to the act of simply looking up, not related to prayer, as in (5a–c):

(5) a. God cwæð ða to Abrame, æfter ðan þe Loth wæs totwæmed him fram: *Ahefe* upp *þine eagan* & beheald fram ðære stowe þe ðu on stenst to norðdæle & to suðdæle & to eastdæle & to westdæle. (Gen 13.14)
   'After Lot and Abram had parted, the Lord said to Abram, "Look around from where you are towards north, south, east and west:' (Gen. 13:14)

b. To þæs stefne se drihtnes wer hraðe *his eagan* upp *ahof* fram þære bocrædingce & locode on þone. (GD 2 (C) 31.164.5)
   'Upon hearing the voice, the man of the Lord quickly raised up his eyes from reading of the book and looked at it.'

c. Þa wæs ymb hwile, ða gefelde he þæt se deada man his leomu ealle astyrede, & *his eagan* up *ahof* & forð locade. (LS 17.1 (MartinMor) 122)
   'After a while, he found that the dead man moved all his limbs, raised up his eyes, and looked around.'

It might be argued that the instances in (5a–c) above exemplify another usage of the gesture in Old English religious texts: one realises something new or important by raising his/her eyes. In (5a), after raising his eyes, the land around Abram would have looked different to him, as something that was already given to him, assured by God's promise. In (5b), the man of God raises his eyes, and at the same time, he perceives the voice from outside. In (5c), the dead man realises that he is alive again by raising his eyes and looking around. It appears, however, that this usage did not gain popularity in Old and Middle English. Nor is it certain if this is directly related to an expansion of the gesture into various contexts in later Middle English, given that no such usage is observable in early Middle English as we will see in Section 3.

The only instance of *to raise one's eyes* to imply arrogance or proudness has been quoted in (2a–c), where *abregdan* is used as well as *hebban*. However, the verse in question is not similarly rendered in the Old English Psalms. For instance, the corresponding verse in the Paris Psalter is cited in (6):

(6) Nis min heorte wið þe ahafen, drihten, ne mine eagan wið þe on *oferhygde*. (PPs 130.1)
'LORD, my heart is not proud, nor are my eyes haughty;' (Ps. 131:1)

Here, *oferhygde* 'haughty' is used instead of *abregdan/hebban eagan* as in (2a–c). As the Vulgate reads 'neque elati sunt oculi mei' ('nor are my eyes elevated'), it would be reasonable to assume that in Benedict's *Rule* the literal translation was adopted, while in the Old English Psalms it was not; therefore, using *to raise one's eyes* to mean 'haughty' did not spread widely.[8]

To summarise, *to raise one's eyes* is used exclusively in religious texts in Old English and has a strong connection with the act of prayer. There existed other usages of the expression, but they remained marginal.

3. Middle English

The data for the Middle English period comes from *Innsbruck Corpus of Middle English Prose* (ICoMEP) (Full version 2.4) (Markus 2010). Instances containing *eien* 'eyen' were searched for,[9] and then those occurring with a verb meaning 'to raise' were manually sorted out. As this corpus only consists of prose texts, *A concordance to Middle English metrical romances* (Saito & Imai 1988), *Piers Plowman: Concordance* (Wittig 2001), and *A concordance to the complete works of Geoffrey Chaucer* (Tatlock & Kennedy 1963) were consulted, too, in an attempt to at least partially supplement the gap between the data from the Old and

---

[8] This does not mean that *to raise one's eyes* was never adopted in English to mean 'haughty.' In the Wycliffite Bible, we read 'ne rerid vp þen myn eȝen' (early) and 'nether myn iȝen ben reisid' (later), and in the Authorized Version, 'not mine eyes loftie.'
[9] The search was made with AntConc (3.4.4) using a regular expression '¥b(i|e|y)[yiehgn3]+n¥b.'

8

Middle English periods.[10]

In the Middle English period, the type of verb collocating with *eyes* changes drastically. In ICoMEP (Table 5), the verb normally collocating with *eyes* in the early part (roughly, up to the thirteenth century) is *heave*, a continuation from the previous period, but in the later part (from the fourteenth century onwards), *lift* begins to occupy that position and is still in current use. What should catch our attention is the variety of verbs occurring with *eyes*. Along with the two verbs just mentioned, we find *cast up, have . . . upwards, hold up, raise up, rear up* and *throw up*. Such variation is seen even within a single text. In *Speculum Sacerdotale*, an early fifteenth-century collection of sermons, as many as four are used: *cast up, lift up, raise up*, and *rear up*—a striking contrast to the uniformity in Old English texts.

Table 5. *V eien* in ICoMEP

Verb	Freq.	Text	Date of
cast up	1	*Life of St. Katherine*	1200+
	2	*Gesta Romanorum*	1400+
	2	*Speculum Sacerdotale*	1400+
have . . . upwards	1	*Cloud of Unknowing and the Book of Privy Counselling*	1500+
heave (up)	2	*Twelfth-Cent. Homilies, Vespasian*	1150+
	4 (7)	*Ancrene Wisse* (Corpus, Gonville, Nero, Pepys)	1200+
	2	*OE Homilies*	a1225
	1 (2)	The Parson's Tale (Skeat, Blake)	c1405
hold up	1 (3)	*Ancrene Wisse* (Corpus, Gonville, Pepys)	1200+

---

[10] However, no instance of *to raise one's eyes* was found in *Metrical romances*.

lift (up)	2	*Lollard Sermons*	a1400
	1	*A Myrour to Lewde Men and Wymmen*	1400+
	1	*Alphabet of Tales*	1400+
	1	*Book of the foundation of St. Bartholomew's Church*	1400+
	1	*Gesta Romanorum*	1400+
	1	Nicholas Love, *Mirror of the Blessed Life of Jesus Christ*	1400+
	1	*Pepysian Gospel Harmony*	1400+
	2	*Speculum Sacerdotale*	1400+
	5	*Richard Rolle of Hampole*	a1450
	1	Caxton, *The Doctrinal of Sapience*	1450+
	1	Caxton, *Quattuor Sermones*	1450+
	1	*Dicts and Saying of the Philosophers*	1450+
	2	*The Revelations of Saint Birgitta*	1450+
	1	*ME Translations of De Imitatione Christi*	a1500
	3	*Cloud of Unknowing and the Book of Privy Counselling*	1500+
	1	*Rule of St. Saviour: Syon Additions for the Sisters*	1500+
	1	*Three Lives from the Gilte Legende*	X
raise up	1	*Speculum Sacerdotale*	1400+
rear up	1	*Speculum Sacerdotale*	1400+
throw up	2	*Testament of Love*	1450+

10

Table 6. The number of text types in ICoMEP in which *V eien* occurs

Religious		Non-religious	
Bible (paraphrase)	1	documents/wills/statutes	1
biography of saints	2	educational fiction	1
fiction (saints' legend)	1	fiction	1
homily	1	philosophy	1
religious, mysticism	1	rules	1
religious, treatise	4		
religious, treatise (contemplative)	1		
religious, treatise / mysticism	1		
religious, treatise / sermon	1		
sermon	3		
sermon (homily)	2		

The context of the gesture's usage in Middle English texts continues to be mostly the same as in Old English texts. As shown in Table 6, *raise one's eyes* is still preferred in religious texts. In the following instances, a woman in prayer raises her eyes and hands up to heaven:[11]

(7) a. FOR þi mi leoue suster sone se þu eauer under3etest þet tes dogge of helle cume . . . ne li þu nawt stille ne ne site nowðer. to lokin hwet he wule don. . . . Rung up sture þe. *hald up ehnen* on heh & honden toward heouene. . . . AD te leuaui oculos meos. leuaui oculos meos in montes. (cnccor 149–50)
'Because of this, my beloved sister, as soon as you understand that this dog of hell comes, do not lie still nor sit to look what he wishes to do. Stand up and move. Raise up your eyes and hands high towards heaven. "I lift my eyes to you" (Ps. 123:1). "IF I lift up my eyes to the hills" (Ps. 121:1).'
   b. she [Mary] kneled done with souereyn deuocion & haldyng vp boþe hire handes & *liftyng vp hire eyen* to heuen seid þees wordes, Lo here þe hande

---

[11] Citation sources in Section 3, unless otherwise stated, refer to the ICoMEP short names.

maiden & þe seruant of my lord be it done to me & fulfilled after þi worde. (mirbles 25–6)

(7a) is quoted from *Ancrene Wisse*, one of the earliest works in Middle English. The anchoress is advised to raise her eyes and hands when she notices the coming of the dog of hell, as told by the psalmist. Likewise, in (7b), Mary kneels down and begins her prayer, lifting her hands and eyes to heaven.

Similarly, in (8), the soul raises his eyes to the angel, a higher being, which evokes a scene of prayer:

(8) And so att ych tyme, the angell of God esed þe paynes; und after ych payne, the sowle *lyft vp his eyn* to the angell, no thing sayng, bot shewyng in his beryng þat he was comforted be him; and þat he shuld hastely be saved. (birgitta 84)

Even in texts not categorised as religious, the scene of prayer is common, as in (9a–b):

(9) a. And so he [Socrates] took Euclites bi the hand & set it on his visage. þen Euclites said to him: Sir, commaunde me whaat that ye wil. And he aunswerd no thing; and then he *lift vp his ien* to heuen & said: I presente my soule to þe maker of alle the worlde; & so deied. And Euclites closed his mouthe and his ien. (dicts 79–80)

   b. whenne þe dowter hurde þis, And sawe þe thre vessellys, she *lifte vp hire yen* to god, and saide, 'Thowe, lord, þat knowist all thing, graunt me þy grace nowe in þe nede of þis tyme, scil. þat I may chese at þis tyme, wherthorowe I may ioy þe sone of þe Emperour, and haue him to husbond.' (gestarom 300)

In (9a), a passage describing the death of Socrates, he raises his eyes to heaven to pray to God to receive his soul. In (9b), too, the daughter raises her eyes to God and prays that she may choose the right vessel.

In later Middle English, however, instances begin to appear without any implication of prayer or the presence of God or other higher beings. An example is given in (10):

(10) he saw a man Rynne afore him, with al the myght of his bodye, & an vnycorne Rynnynge aftir him, wher thorowe the man was gretly a-dredde, that for fer he felle in to a gret diche. neuer þe les he toke holde by a tree . . . & then he lokid downe, & he saw at the fote of the tree an hidowse pitte, and an orible dragon þere in. . . . He *cast vp his yen*, and he saw a passage of hony fallyng fro braunche to braunche; & he sette his herte so muche to this swete syght of hony, þat he forgate that oþere perell. (gestarom 110)

The man falls into a great ditch but barely saves himself by holding on to a tree. He then looks down to find a horrible dragon at the foot of the tree, but when he raises his eyes, he finds honey falling from branch to branch. His heart is so occupied with the honey that he forgets the danger of the dragon beneath him. In this context, it might be said that the act of looking up serves to imply hope, ease, or comfort. But such usage is too rare in the ICoMEP data to describe and analyse the expansion of *to raise one's eyes* into contexts other than prayer.

Table 7. *To raise one's eyes* in Chaucer's verse

Title/line		Verb	Title/line		Verb
CT	MLT 840	*heave up*		III, 183	*throw up*
	NPT 4383	*cast up*		IV, 1159	*throw upward*
	MerT 2360	*cast up*		V, 1159	*heave up*
BD	212	*cast up*	*HF*	I, 495	*cast (to heaven)*
TC	I, 726	*cast up*		III, 318	*cast up*
	II, 971	*throw up*		III, 1062	*cast up*

In Chaucer's works, however, instances of *to raise one's eyes* without any religious implication are not uncommon.[12] Of the twelve instances of the expression in Chaucer's verse (Table 7),[13] nine are used as such. In

---

[12] Chaucer has 'traditional' usage of the gesture as well in the Parson's Tale (986), which refers to the parable of the Pharisee and the tax-collector in Luke 18:13 as in (3b).

[13] One more instance is found in prose works (the Parson's Tale; Table 5).

some cases, the gesture seems to serve as a literary device to draw the reader's attention to the development of the story, two of which are shown in (11):[14]

(11) a. For, certes, swete, I am but ded.
Ye shul me never on lyve yse.
. . . . ,
With that *hir eyen up* she *casteth*
And saw noght. 'Allas!' quod she for sorwe,
And deyede within the thridde morwe. (*BD* 204–5, 212–14)
b. Bifel that Chauntecleer in al his pryde,
His sevene wyves walkynge by his syde,
Caste up his eyen to the brighte sonne,
That in the signe of Taurus hadde yronne
Twenty degrees and oon, and somwhat moore,
And knew by kynde, and by noon oother loore,
That it was pryme, and crew with blisful stevene. (NPT 4381–7)

In (11a), *to raise one's eyes* vividly marks the change of the state Alcyone is in—from illusion to disillusion. Alcyone, in her dream, is told by her husband Ceyx that he is dead. Upon hearing this, she returns to reality—she raises her eyes up and awakes, but sees nothing. She is overwhelmed by sorrow and dies within three days. In (11b), the gesture rather ironically highlights the time of day when something sorrowful happens to Chanticleer the cock. He, walking with his seven wives, raises his eyes to the sun to know by instinct that it is nine o'clock and crows with a happy voice, but is not aware that this happy time of the day is also the time when his fate is sealed. At the very same time, Russell the fox is lying in ambush for Chanticleer and his cunning trick ends in success (ll. 4521–7). This usage might be comparable to (5a–c) in the previous section in that the gesture is used as a signal to introduce some new, important information to the story. (We will return to Chaucer's usage of the gesture in the next section.)

In *Piers Plowman* there is only one instance of *to raise one's eyes*, cited

---

[14] Quotations from Chaucer are taken from Benson (2008).

14

in (12), which is also unconnected to prayer:[15]

(12) And as I *caste vp myn eyghen* · one loked on me, and axed
Of me, what thinge it were? · 'ywisse, sire,' I seide, (B, XI, 400–1)

In this passage, the dreamer awakes from his dream and, as he raises his eyes, notices someone above him asking him what he learned about 'Dowel' in the dream. The gesture is presumably used to introduce the new character whose name is later revealed as 'Ymagynatyf' (B, XII, 1), a usage similar to Chaucer's mentioned above in (11a–b).[16]

Three main findings from the Middle English data can be summarised thus: first, the verb describing the gesture changes drastically. *To heave,* which was the norm in Old English, continued to be so until early Middle English but eventually began to be superseded by a variety of verbs, among which *to lift* became the new norm. Second, the usage of the gesture in the context of prayer continues to be dominant. This is observed not only in religious texts but also in secular texts. Third, a change in usage is also observed. It takes place in the later part of the period. The expanded range of usage is particularly evident in Chaucer.

4. Discussion

In the previous two sections, we have seen that *to raise one's eyes* was mostly used to describe a scene of prayer, but in later Middle English, especially in the language of Chaucer, it began to express something more than prayer. Based on the data provided above, this section explores why the gesture was so closely related to prayer and how its range of usage expanded.

To begin with, it is quite reasonable to say that the usage of *to raise one's eyes* in contexts related to prayer is ultimately traceable back to the Bible. According to Shackleford (2000: 43), it is 'One of the most common of biblical phrases concerning the seeing eye' and its usage is abundant in

---

[15] Quotations from *Piers Plowman* are taken from Skeat (1886).
[16] However, the corresponding lines in the C-text simply read: 'And thenne was ther a wiȝt · what he was ich nuste:— / "What ys Dowel?" quath that wiȝt · "y-wys, syre," ich seyde,' (C, XIV, 220–1).

both the Old and New Testaments. He concludes that:

(13) To me, 'lifting up the eyes' has a significance that is not implied by the
action of simply, 'looking up.' Indeed, 'lifting the eyes,' in almost every
instance of its use in the Bible, presages some important event, action, or in
some way prepares the reader for the recognition of a momentous reality.
(Shackleford 2000: 44)

Although Shackleford's conclusion seems rather impressionistic since he
does not cite any statistical details, it is true that most occurrences of *to
raise one's eyes* in Old and Middle English texts surveyed are more or
less related to biblical contexts, especially prayer, as shown in Sections 2
and 3. It is thus a natural assumption that the phrase *to raise one's eyes*
was in some way transported into English literature from the Bible.
However, a question may arise: among different usages of *to raise one's
eyes* in the Bible, why is it only the one related to prayer that is repeatedly
found in early English texts?

The answer may lie in the relationship between gesture and prayer in
medieval times in Christian contexts—prayer was not just read but also
performed. Jorgensen (2016), in her discussion of Anglo-Saxons learning
emotion scripts from gestures described in the Psalms, states that 'The
Psalms are emotion scripts in the literal sense that they tell people what to
say: they are not simply for reading and comprehending but for praying
and performing' (128). As regards the gesture of raising eyes in prayer,
Jorgensen, referring to an illustration in the Paris Psalter manuscript
(Paris, Bibliothèque Nationale, lat. 8824), argues that:

(14) The idea of needy petition is reinforced in the manuscript by the interlinear
drawing that fills in space beneath the Latin text of [Psalm 5] v. 5. The
psalmist, hands spread out in supplication and face turned upwards with an
anxious expression, gazes towards God's hand, which emerges out of the
clouds holding a pair of dividers symbolic of His creative power. . . .
(Jorgensen 2016: 136)

In a similar vein, Robertson (2003: 129), discussing how *Ancrene Wisse*
was read, points out that 'the recitation of these prayers [in Part 1 of

16

Ancrene Wisse] involves a bodily performance.' She goes on to say that:

(15) Part 1 . . . describes the bodily positions that must accompany these prayers. . . . Virtually every prayer is accompanied by a physical action, such as prostration, kneeling, or the raising of head or hands. The anchoress is told to enact the very variety of bodily positions in prayer that we see displayed in Peter the Chanter's *The Christian at Prayer* [(Trexler 1987)]. . . . (Robertson 2003: 129–30)

These views may help explain the frequent use of *to raise one's eyes* in the scene of prayer. When bodily performances were inseparable from prayer, it would have been natural to include such gestures in descriptions of prayer. For those engaged in religious services in particular, it would have worked as a guide in offering prayer as Robertson suggests. Apart from such limited contexts, too, the description of gestures would have made it easy for the reader or listener to imagine the scene of prayer in his/her mind. It thus seems safe to say that the close association between prayer and gestures led to the extensive use of *to raise one's eyes* in religious texts especially in reference to prayer.

Such repeated use of *to raise one's eyes* eventually led to its expansion into non-Christian contexts as in (9a–b), and furthermore into contexts unrelated to prayer as in (10), (11a–b), and (12). The expansion is manifest in Chaucer as briefly mentioned in the last part of the previous section. Since Chaucer's use of gesture has attracted much scholarly attention, it seems fruitful to focus on his use of *to raise one's eyes* in order to shed light on the expansion of the phrase into new contexts.[17] Windeatt (1979: 143) observes that 'Chaucer's most persistent interest in gesture . . . centers on the eyes and faces of his characters and their acts of

---

[17] It is worth noting that 'Habicht [(1959)] says that the directed gaze is itself an unusual gesture in Middle English poetry' (Benson 1980: 33). In the texts surveyed for the present study, too, no instance of *to raise one's eyes* was found in *Metrical romances* (n. 10) and only one instance in *Pierse Plowman*. Considering these facts, although it would be too hasty to conclude that Chaucer was the first author to introduce the new usage of *to raise one's eyes* into English literature, it would not be too much to say that his creativity in using the expression is ahead of the times.

looking.' Although Windeatt does not lay special emphasis on the gesture of raising eyes, Benson (1980) carefully deals with and interprets almost every occurrence of that gesture in *Troilus and Criseyde*, which in his words 'must be regarded as his [Chaucer's] best work' (82) to study gesture in Chaucer. In *Troilus and Criseyde* there are five instances of *to raise one's eyes* as quoted in (16a–e), which in fact account for nearly half of the total occurrences of the gesture in Chaucer's verse (Table 7):

(16) a. And sith thow woost I do it for no wyle,
　　　And sith I am he that thow trustest moost,
　　　Tel me somwhat, syn al my wo thow woost.'
　　　Yet Troilus for al this no word seyde,
　　　But longe he ley as stylle as he ded were;
　　　And after this with sikynge he abreyde,
　　　And to Pandarus vois he lente his ere,
　　　And *up his eighen caste* he, that in feere
　　　Was Pandarus, lest that in frenesie
　　　He sholde falle, or elles soone dye; (I, 719–28)
　　b. Right so gan tho *his eighen up* to *throwe*
　　　This Troilus, and seyde, 'O Venus deere,
　　　Thi myght, thi grace, yheried be it here!' (II, 971–3)
　　c. Fil Pandarus on knees, and *up his eyen*
　　　To heven *threw*, and held his hondes highe:
　　　'Immortal god,' quod he, 'that mayst nought deyen,
　　　Cupide I mene, of this mayst glorifie;
　　　And Venus, thow mayst maken melodie! (III, 183–7)
　　d. And thus she lith with hewes pale and grene,
　　　That whilom fressh and fairest was to sene.
　　　This Troilus, that on hire gan biholde,
　　　Clepyng hire name — and she lay as for ded —
　　　Without answere, and felte hire lymes colde,
　　　Hire eyen throwen upward to hire hed, (IV, 1154–9)
　　e. 'We han naught elles for to don, ywis.
　　　And Pandarus, now woltow trowen me?
　　　Have here my trouthe, I se hire! Yond she is!
　　　Heve up thyn eyen, man! Maistow nat se?'
　　　Pandare answerde, 'Nay, so mote I the!

Al wrong, by God! What saistow, man? Where arte?
That I se yond nys but a fare-carte.' (V, 1156–62)

In (16a), *to raise one's eyes* is among the series of gestures depicting Troilus' lovesickness in detail (cf. Benson 1980: 88). Troilus, without saying a word, lies as still as if he were dead, then awakes with a sigh, lends his ear to Pandarus, and raises his eyes. Pandarus, seeing this, fears that Troilus could soon fall in a frenzy or even die. On the contrary, in (16b), the same gesture describes Troilus praising Venus when he hears from Pandarus that Criseyde will love him (Benson 1980: 91), a vivid expression of his great rejoicing. Here, the gesture is related to prayer, but it is no longer something performed by the reader as was the case in the Psalms (Jorgensen 2016) or *Ancrene Wisse* (Robertson 2003) mentioned above. In Book III, Pandarus parodies this gesture as in (16c) (Benson 1980: 91, n. 15). Just after Criseyde embraces and kisses Troilus, Pandarus falls on his knees and raises his eyes and hands to heaven to praise Cupid and Venus, a series of gestures expressing 'Pandarus' delight in the success of his scheming' (Benson 1980: 93). In (16d), the gesture is employed as a means of, in Benson's words (1980: 98), graphically depicting Criseyde's swoon. Chaucer is not content with a simple description of her swoon but adds its details: her face is pale, her limbs are cold, she is lying as if dead, and her eyes are raised upwards in her head. Benson (1980: 98) argues that this detailed description is necessary 'because in reaction to her swoon, Troilus, thinking Criseyde is dead, nearly kills himself.' The last instance of *to raise one's eyes* in (16e) is not dealt with by Benson, but Jimura (2005: 61) refers to this passage in his discussion on the function of the house, including the walls, in the work. According to him, 'the walls between the two armies that separate this [Criseyde's] palace from Criseyde's Greek camp are also the walls that alienate Troilus from Criseyde' (Jimura 2005: 58). In (16e), the walls function as such: Troilus, looking beyond the walls, thinks that he has seen Criseyde coming back, but actually it is an illusion as Pandarus answers. Although Jimura (2005: 61) does not explicitly mention the particular gesture in question, it might be argued that Troilus' reference to the gesture emphasises his excitement at seeing Criseyde[18] and his eagerness to call Pandarus' attention to her coming back. Carefully considering these five instances in *Troilus and Criseyde*, it appears safe to say that Chaucer's effective usage of *to raise one's eyes* indicates that the gesture expanded its range of expression as a literary device. It might also be said that Chaucer's usage of the gesture is highly similar to those we encounter in present-day literature as in (1a–b).

By way of summary, this section has sought answers to the two questions raised in the opening paragraph. As to the first question, *to raise one's eyes* was frequently used to describe a scene of prayer because of the strong connection between prayer and gesture. Description of the gesture of raising eyes, along with other gestures, helped the reader not only read but also perform the prayer. As to the second question, it appears that the repeated use of *to raise one's eyes* to describe Christian prayer eventually led to its expansion into new contexts, including non-Christian prayer and passages unrelated to prayer at all. The expanded usage of the gesture is especially observable in Chaucer, who used it as a literary device to highlight the development of the story or to describe emotions or appearances of the characters in detail.

5. Final Remarks

This paper has dealt with the usage of *to raise one's eyes* in Old and Middle English by scrutinising data from various texts and authors. When this gesture is used in Old and Middle English literature, it is mostly a description of a scene of prayer because such passages often served to tell people how to perform the prayer. The strong association of raising eyes and prayer led to expanded usage of the gesture in later Middle English. The expression began to be applied not only to Christian prayer, but also non-Christian prayer and even contexts utterly unrelated to prayer. In later Middle English, especially in the language of Chaucer, the usage was very similar to today's usage, leading to the enrichment of literary expressiveness in the English language.

---

[18] Jimura (in a personal communication) has a view similar to my own. He comments that for Troilus, it is as if there is a sudden halo of light and his earnest love for Criseyde is rewarded.

20

References

Benson, Larry D. (ed.). 2008. *The Riverside Chaucer*. 3rd ed., with a new foreword by Christopher Cannon. Oxford: Oxford University Press.

Benson, Robert G. 1980. *Medieval body language: A study of the use of gesture in Chaucer's poetry*. Copenhagen: Rosenkilde and Bagger.

BNC Online. <http://scnweb.jkn21.com/BNC2/>.

Cook, Albert S. 1903. *Biblical quotations in Old English prose writers*. New York: Charles Scribner's Sons.

Forshall, Josiah & Frederic Madden (eds.). 1850. *The Holy Bible: Containing the Old and New Testaments, with the Apocryphal Books, in the earliest English versions made from the Latin Vulgate by John Wycliffe and his followers*. Reprinted by New York: AMS Press, 1982.

Habichit, Werner. 1959. *Die Gebärde in englischen Dichtungen des Mittelalters*. Munich: Verlag der Bayerische Akademie der Wissenschaften.

Healey, Antonette diPaolo (ed.). 2000. *The Dictionary of Old English corpus*. Toronto: Dictionary of Old English Project. <http://ota.ox.ac.uk/desc/ 2488>.

Jimura, Akiyuki. 2005. *Studies in Chaucer's words and his narratives*. Hiroshima: Keisuisha.

Jorgensen, Alice. 2016. Learning about emotion from the Old English prose Psalm of the Paris Psalter. In Alice Jorgensen, Frances McCormack, & Jonathan Wilcox (eds.), *Anglo-Saxon emotions: Reading the heart in Old English language, literature and culture*, 127–42. London: Routledge.

Markus, Manfred (ed.). 2010. *Innsbruck corpus of Middle English prose*. Version 2.4. Innsbruck: The English Department of the University of Innsbruck.

Robertson, Elizabeth. 2003. Savoring 'scientia.' In Yoko Wada (ed.), *A companion to* Ancrene Wisse, 113–44. Cambridge: D. S. Brewer.

Saito, Toshio & Mitsunori Imai (eds.). 1988. *A concordance to Middle English metrical romances*. Frankfurt am Main: Verlag Peter Lang.

Shackleford, John M. 2000. *Biblical body language: The figurative face of Scripture*. Lanham, Maryland: University Press of America.

Skeat, Walter W. (ed.) 1886. *The vision of William concerning Piers Plowman*. Oxford: Oxford University Press.

Tatlock, John S. P. & Arthur G. Kennedy. 1963. *A concordance to the complete works of Geoffrey Chaucer and to the Romaunt of the rose*. Gloucester, Mass.: Peter Smith.

The Holy Bible: An exact reprint in roman type, page for page of the Authorized Version published in the year 1611. With an introduction by Alfred W. Pollard. Reprinted by Oxford: Oxford University Press / Tokyo: Kenkyusha, 1985.

The Revised English Bible with Apocrypha. Oxford: Oxford University Press / Cambridge: Cambridge University Press, 1989.

Trexler, Richard C. 1987. *The Christian at prayer: An illustrated prayer manual attributed to Peter the Chanter (d. 1197).* New York: Medieval and Renaissance Texts and Studies.

Weber. Robert & Roger Gryson (eds.). 2007. *Biblia sacra iuxta Vulgatam versionem.* 5th ed. Stuttgart: Deutsche Bibelgesellschaft.

Windeatt, Barry 1979. Gesture in Chaucer. *Medievalia et humanistica* 9, 143–61.

Wittig, Joseph S. 2001. *Piers Plowman: Concordance, Will's visions of Piers Plowman. Do-well, Do-better and Do-best.* London: The Athlone Press.

The Use of 'Hand(s)' in Shakespeare's Romance Plays

Noritaka Tomimura

1. Introduction

Body language in drama is important in two aspects: performance and text. First, dramatic works are written to be performed on stage, and acting inevitably involves body movement. For example, actors need to walk from the wings in order to appear on stage. Appropriate gestures are needed to express character feelings such as love, hate, fear, anger and surprise. Second, texts spoken by actors contain references to body parts just as novels and poems do. This aspect is particularly significant in order to understand the different characteristics of plays and narrative texts.

This article deals with the use of 'hand(s)' in Shakespeare's plays. One reason for focusing on that specific part of the body is that 'hand' is the most frequently used word among words related to body language. Figure 1 shows the frequencies of nouns that refer to particular body areas.[1]

---

[1] This data was acquired from WordHoard, an application which was developed by Northwestern University and contains tagged digital texts of the Shakespeare canon. WordHoard enables easier examination of the playwrights' use of words by parts of speech, although some errors remain in its tagging. Aside from this application, several comprehensive concordances to Shakespeare have been compiled: *The Complete Concordance to Shakespeare* by Mary Cowden Clarke, which was first published between 1844 and 1845, John Bartlett's *A Complete Concordance or Verbal Index to Words, Phrases and Passages in the Dramatic Works of Shakespeare* in 1894, and Marvin Spevack's *A Complete and Systematic*

Among them, the number of occurrences of hand (or hands) amounts to 1119 in total. This suggests that the hand is regarded as an important part of the body, and is thus frequently referred to, either because of the playwright's dramatic intention or out of some necessity. Another reason is that the hand is important not only in the dialogue, as we have just observed, but also in the actual gestures of actors. Various types of actions performed on stage, from giving something to another actor to stabbing a character to death, involve hand movements. Furthermore, in most cases these hand movements are visible to the audience. In contrast, movements and appearance of 'eye(s),' the second most common word shown in Figure 1, are generally difficult for the audience to notice. Accordingly, the range of functions that eyes can carry out on stage in terms of body language is less broad. Hands are more capable of expressing notions or ideas in the dialogue and of presenting direct and actual movements to the audience. For these reasons, this paper examines the use of 'hand(s)' in Shakespeare's plays.

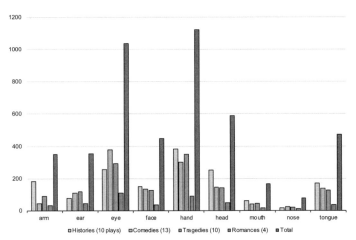

Figure 1. Frequencies of nouns concerning body language in Shakespeare's 37 plays[2]

Concordance to the Works of Shakespeare. However, none of these provides frequencies of words by parts of speech.

[2] Plays included in each genre are as follows. Estimated first performance dates

2. Modifiers Used with 'Hand(s)'

To begin with, let us observe the modifiers used with 'hand(s).' Modifiers can appear either before or after the core noun 'hand(s),' but this study concentrates on the modifiers found immediately before 'hand(s)' for the sake of clarity.

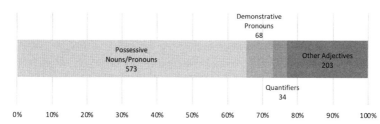

Figure 2. Types and frequencies of modifiers occurring directly before 'hand(s)' in Shakespeare's 37 plays

Figure 2 gives the frequencies of each type of modifier that show up one word before 'hand(s)' in Shakespeare's 37 plays.[3] The most frequently observed group of modifiers consists of possessive nouns and pronouns. Table 1 gives the frequencies of each possessive noun and

---

in parentheses are based on Harbage (1989). Histories: *Henry VI Part 1* (1590), *Henry VI Part 2* (1590), *Henry VI Part 3* (1591), *King John* (1591), *Richard III* (1592), *Richard II* (1595), *Henry IV Part 1* (1597), *Henry IV Part 2* (1597), *Henry V* (1599), *Henry VIII* (1613); Comedies: *The Comedy of Errors* (1592), *The Taming of the Shrew* (1592), *The Two Gentlemen of Verona* (1593), *Love's Labour's Lost* (1595), *A Midsummer Night's Dream* (1596), *The Merchant of Venice* (1596), *The Merry Wives of Windsor* (1597), *Much Ado about Nothing* (1598), *As You Like It* (1599), *Twelfth Night* (1601), *Troilus and Cressida* (1602), *All's Well That Ends Well* (1603), *Measure for Measure* (1604); Tragedies: *Titus Andronicus* (1594), *Romeo and Juliet* (1596), *Julius Caesar* (1599), *Hamlet* (1601), *Othello* (1604), *King Lear* (1605), *Macbeth* (1606), *Antony and Cleopatra* (1607), *Timon of Athens* (1607), *Coriolanus* (1608); Romances: *Pericles* (1608), *Cymbeline* (1609), *The Winter's Tale* (1610), *The Tempest* (1611).

[3] Hereafter, analyses are performed using AntConc, a concordancer developed by Anthony Laurence, and the digital texts of *Shakespeare's Plays, Sonnets and Poems* from Folger Digital Texts as the primary texts. All examples are checked manually and words that belong to other word classes, such as verbs and prepositions, are excluded from the statistics.

pronoun in this group, and it is easily noticeable that the first and second person pronouns 'your,' 'my,' and 'thy' are dominant. This suggests that when hands are referred to in dialogue they often directly designate those of the characters engaged in the conversation. A similar tendency can be observed in the use of demonstrative pronouns, which constitute the second largest group in Figure 2. Table 2 provides the frequencies of each demonstrative pronoun and makes clear that the use of 'this' predominates over other pronouns. This implies that hands either of the speaker or other characters nearby on stage are frequently indicated with demonstrative pronouns. To summarize, the word 'hand(s)' appears very often in the context of describing the hands of characters involved in the dialogue taking place on the stage.

In contrast, the proportion of other adjectives is rather small, amounting to about 20%. However, a closer analysis of this group enables us to examine another aspect of the use of 'hand(s).' Table 3 shows the frequencies of adjectives excluding quantifiers. An interesting character-istic which draws attention is the variety of adjectives. There are 126 different adjectives for the 203 instances of 'hand(s)' (see Figure 2). Apart from the most frequently used adjective 'right,' the number of instances of each adjective is less than 10. Figure 3 further clarifies this characteristic, showing that about 80% of the adjectives are used only once before 'hand(s)' in Shakespeare's 37 plays. These observations suggest that the ways the adjectives modify 'hand(s)' are closely tied with specific con-texts in which 'hand(s)' are used, and repetition of the same combinations of 'adjective + hand(s)' is generally avoided.

Table 1. Frequencies of possessive nouns/pronouns one word before 'hand(s)'

Rank	Word	Token
1	your	132
2	my	100
3	thy	91
4	his	75
5	's *	59
6	her	39
7	their	25

8	our	23
9	own	15
10	highness'	3
11	diomedes'	1
11	hastings'	1
11	justices'	1
11	laertes'	1
11	martius'	1
11	pilgrims'	1
11	posthumus'	1
11	soldiers'	1
11	titus'	1
11	traitors'	1
11	venus'	1

* 's means the possessive case as in 'King Richard's hand.'

Table 2. Frequencies of demonstrative pronouns one word before 'hand(s)'

Rank	Word	Token
1	this	44
2	these	12
3	that	10
4	those	2

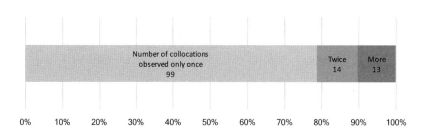

Figure 3. Ratio of collocations found only once in Shakespeare's 37 plays

28

Table 3. Frequencies of adjectives except quantifiers observed immediately before 'hand(s)'[4]

No.	Rank	Word	Token	No.	Rank	Word	Token
1	1	right	16	36	28	bounteous	1
2	2	white	8	37	28	bow	1
3	3	bloody	7	38	28	buried	1
4	3	good	7	39	28	charitable	1
5	5	fair(er, est)	5	40	28	civil	1
6	5	left	5	41	28	clean	1
7	5	royal	5	42	28	cold	1
8	5	strong(est)	5	43	28	collateral	1
9	5	violent	5	44	28	conqu'ring	1
10	10	heavy	4	45	28	court	1
11	11	gracious	3	46	28	coward	1
12	11	rude	3	47	28	cruel	1
13	11	very	3	48	28	cunning	1
14	14	chopped	2	49	28	dainty	1
15	14	cursed	2	50	28	damned	1
16	14	dry	2	51	28	deformed	1
17	14	fatal	2	52	28	desperate	1
18	14	fierce	2	53	28	dirty	1
19	14	hard	2	54	28	disjoining	1
20	14	kingly	2	55	28	even	1
21	14	noble	2	56	28	false	1
22	14	open	2	57	28	favorable	1
23	14	proper	2	58	28	favoring	1
24	14	purpled	2	59	28	feeble	1
25	14	sweet	2	60	28	fine	1
26	14	victorious	2	61	28	flower-soft	1
27	14	weak(er)	2	62	28	foremost	1
28	28	accursed	1	63	28	foul	1
29	28	aiding	1	64	28	freestone-colored	1
30	28	armed	1	65	28	friendly	1
31	28	banished	1	66	28	full	1
32	28	bare	1	67	28	gentle	1
33	28	bastard	1	68	28	gilded	1
34	28	bawdy	1	:	:	:	:
35	28	boist'rous	1	126	28	withered	1

---

[4] Instances of different meanings such as 'a person's handwriting' are included in this table.

We have examined some overall tendencies regarding the use of 'hand(s)' in the Shakespeare canon. Keeping these observations in mind, let us take a closer look at some specific examples. In the following sections, I would like to focus on the instances found in Shakespeare's romance plays *Pericles (Per.)*, *Cymbeline (Cym.)*, *The Winter's Tale (WT)* and *The Tempest (Tem.)*, because these plays were presumably written during a relatively short period around the end of Shakespeare's career, and thus are expected to reveal some tendencies which are characteristic of this genre.

3. Adjectives Used with 'Hand(s)' in Shakespeare's Romance Plays
In this section, we will examine the examples of adjectives in Shakespeare's romance plays. The adjectives that appear in these plays are: bloody, full, good, heavy, kingly, nimble, proper, sweet, weak, white.[5] First, the adjective 'proper' constitutes the category 'ownership' by itself because the adjective primarily means 'own,' placing an emphasis on the ownership of the hand. Next, the remaining adjectives can be divided into two large groups according to whether they describe visual characteristics or not. These two categories of adjectives are categorized as 'visual characteristics' and 'nonvisual characteristics' respectively. Each group has several subcategories as shown in Table 4. Now let us take a closer look at the examples in these categories.

Table 4. Types of adjectives used with 'hand(s)' in Shakespeare's romance plays

Types	Adjectives
Visual Characteristics	
Static	bloody, white
Dynamic	nimble
Nonvisual Characteristics	
Strength	weak
Value Judgment	good
Social Class	kingly
Other	heavy, full, sweet
Ownership	proper

---

[5] Although the adjective 'right' appears once in the lines of Autolycus in *The Winter's Tale*, it is excluded from the list because the 'hand' in this example is used to indicate a direction or a way and thus has only limited relevance to this study. The lines read: 'Walk before toward the / seaside. Go on the **right hand**. I will but look upon / the hedge, and follow you'. (4.4.957–9)

30

3.1. Visual Characteristics
Adjectives in this category attach concrete visual images to the 'hand(s)' after these modifiers. They are further divided into two subcategories: static and dynamic.

(a) Static
Typical examples of static visual images found in Shakespeare's romance plays are 'white' and 'bloody,' both of which are related to color. In *The Winter's Tale*, Leontes, the King of Sicilia, describes the hand of Hermione, his wife:

(1) LEONTES. Why, that was when
 Three crabbèd months had soured themselves to
 death
 Ere I could make thee open thy **white hand**
 [And] clap thyself my love; then didst thou utter
 'I am yours forever.' (*WT* 1.2.129–34)

Here we can surmise that the queen's hand is, to some extent, literally white. The meaning of the other adjective 'bloody' in the following passage from *Cymbeline* is not as direct as 'white' because the 'hands' referred to here are not necessarily smeared with blood at this particular instant.

(2) CYMBELINE. [. . .] Set on there. Never was a war did cease,
 Ere **bloody hands** were washed, with such a peace.
 (*Cym.* 5.5.585–6)

However, the main connotation here is that the owners of the hands are involved in killing or wounding in a war. Although there is such a difference, both examples of 'hand(s)' embody a strong visual image brought by the adjectives 'white' and 'bloody.'

(b) Dynamic
The term 'dynamic' is applied to the adjectives that portray visible features with kinetic elements. Only one example is found in the four

plays dealt with:

(3) AUTOLYCUS. I understand the business; I hear it. To have
     an open ear, a quick eye, and a **nimble hand** is
     necessary for a cutpurse; (*WT* 4.4.793–5)

The adjective 'nimble' primarily depicts the agility of the hand, but the image of dexterity expands from the body part to the personality of the owner together with other descriptions around the adjective.

3.2. Nonvisual Characteristics
Adjectives that signify nonvisual characteristics are subdivided into four categories: strength, value judgment, social class, and others.

(c) Strength
Hands are often modified by adjectives that show their strength or weakness because they are the major parts of the body used for exercising physical force. In the romance plays of Shakespeare, however, we can find only one example. Imogen describes her weakness when asking Pisanio to kill herself in *Cymbeline*:

(4) IMOGEN.   Why, I must die,
     And if I do not by thy hand, thou art
     No servant of thy master's. Against self-slaughter
     There is a prohibition so divine
     That cravens my **weak hand**. Come, here's my heart—
                                    (*Cym.* 3.4.81–5)

The adjective 'weak' mainly suggests Imogen's physical incapacity to commit suicide, but combined with the reference to the religious notion before, the adjective also implies the lack of mental strength at the same time. This passage can be considered as another example which shows that the feature of hands can imply the character's personality.

(d) Value Judgment
The manifold meanings of 'good' make it difficult to categorize the

32

adjective, but in many cases the speakers' judgments about something according to their standards are involved. The only example is found at the end of *The Tempest*:

(5) PROSPERO. But release me from my bands
       With the help of your **good hands**. (*Tem.* Epilogue 9–10)

This example is somewhat complex because the 'hand' in this passage can mean 'a round of applause.'[6] In this case, 'good' is closer to an intensifier in terms of its function. It seems also possible to construe the word 'hand' as a reference to the body parts of the audience, and 'good' as a description of, or a hope for, the kindness of the owner of the hand, which may give the actor a warm applause.

(e) Social Class
Adjectives can also signify the social status of the owner of the hand. In *Pericles*, Marina narrates the episode of her father Pericles:

(6) MARINA. My father, as nurse says, did never fear,
       But cried 'Good seamen!' to the sailors,
       Galling his **kingly hands** haling ropes,
       And, clasping to the mast, endured a sea
       That almost burst the deck. (*Per.* 4.1.62–6)

The focus of the adjective is rather on the personal characteristics worthy of a monarch than the appearance of the hands itself. This is regarded as another example of an adjective that depicts the personality of the character to whom the hand belongs.

(f) Other
Included in this category are the adjectives 'sweet,' 'heavy,' and 'full.' 'Sweet' appears in the following line by Cloten in *Cymbeline*.

(7) CLOTEN. Good morrow, fairest sister. Your **sweet hand**. (*Cym.* 2.3.99)

---

[6] *OED2* s.v. Hand n.15.

Cloten's words show that the hand of his sister Imogen has some pleasant qualities, but his chief intention is presumably to demonstrate his affection towards his sister. As we have observed in other examples such as 'kingly,' the adjective 'sweet' is used to describe the whole personality of the character.

The two instances below are unique in that the hands belong to personified figures:

(8) CYMBELINE.   Well,
       My peace we will begin. And, Caius Lucius,
       Although the victor, we submit to Caesar
       And to the Roman Empire, promising
       To pay our wonted tribute, from the which
       We were dissuaded by our wicked queen,
       Whom heavens in justice both on her and hers
       Have laid most **heavy hand**. (*Cym.* 5.5.558–65)

(9) CLEON. This Tarsus, o'er which I have the government,
       A city on whom Plenty held **full hand**,
       For Riches strewed herself even in her streets; (*Per.* 1.4.21–3)

The adjectives 'heavy' and 'full' are considered to illustrate the states brought about by each owner of the hand, 'heavens' and 'Plenty.' 'Heavy' in the example 8 refers not to the physical quality of the hand but to the results that the hand—to be more precise, the will of 'heavens'—yielded. Likewise, 'full' in Cleon's account in the example 9 mainly describes the prosperity of the city. These instances show that the adjectives used with 'hand(s)' extend their range of modification to the owner of the hands even when describing non-human figures.

3.3. Ownership
The only adjective that constitutes this category, 'proper,' occurs in the following two passages:

(10) CLOTEN.   Die the death!
       When I have slain thee with my **proper hand**,

I'll follow those that even now fled hence
And on the gates of Lud's Town set your heads.
Yield, rustic mountaineer! (*Cym.* 4.2.128–32)

(11) LEONTES. [. . .] The bastard brains with these my **proper hands**
Shall I dash out. Go, take it to the fire,
For thou sett'st on thy wife. (*WT* 2.3.175–7)

In both examples, the owners of the hand are in wrath and show an open hostility to other characters. It can be said that this adjective of emphasis is typically used when aggressive intention is overt.

To sum up, the observations in this section reveal that the adjectives used with hand(s) in Shakespeare's romance plays serve to express three sets of characteristics regarding hands. Furthermore, most examples show that the adjectives depict not only the physical qualities of the hand itself but also the personal characteristics of the owner of the hand. In other words, there seems to be a tendency toward the metonymical use of the word hand.[7]

4. Gestures with Explicit References to 'Hand(s)'

This section focuses on the actual gestures made by hands. Farah Karim-Cooper argues that there are several types of cues for gestures, and gives relevant examples (2016: 79–81). Most explicitly, the use of gestures is indicated through stage directions such as '*It spreads his arms*' (SD1.1.139.1) in *Hamlet*. The second way of signifying bodily actions is to describe them in the characters' lines. One example is found in act 1 scene 1 in *Romeo and Juliet*, where the characters talk about biting a thumb. Finally, demonstrative pronouns such as 'this' and 'that' can

---

[7] It may be possible to use the term 'synecdochical' here, but Seto (1999: 113–14) differentiates synecdoche from metonymy arguing that synecdoche is 'defined as the C-related transfer, i.e., the categorical transfer based on the semantic inclusion between a more comprehensive and a less comprehensive category.' On the other hand, Littlemore (2015: 23) states that '[. . .] when we look at examples of PART FOR WHOLE relationships in real-world linguistic data, the distinction between metonymy and "synecdoche" becomes very blurred.' Taking these opinions into consideration, I employ the term 'metonymic' in this paper.

suggest the use of gestures. Among the examples Farah Karim-Cooper presents is the line spoken by King Lear: '[*pointing to the map*] Of all these bounds, even from this line to this' (1.1.69). It is possible that the actor moves his fingers to indicate certain areas on the map.

Similar examples are found in Shakespeare's romance plays. In this section, I would like to look at some examples that explicitly refer to hand(s) in the dialogue. They are divided into the context in which certain hand gestures are supposed to be employed.

(a) Reciprocation of Love
The following scenes depict the confirmation of the love between man and woman. In the first example, Ferdinand possibly holds out his hand to Miranda, and she grasps his hand to show that she accepts his love.

(12) FERDINAND. My mistress, dearest, and I thus humble ever.
    MIRANDA. My husband, then?
    FERDINAND.   Ay, with a heart as willing
      As bondage e'er of freedom. **Here's my hand**.
    MIRANDA. [*clasping his hand*]
      And mine, with my heart in 't. And now farewell
      Till half an hour hence. (*Tem*. 3.1.104–9)

The other example is from *Pericles*. Simonides, the king of Pentapolis, confirms the love between Thaisa, his daughter, and Pericles by joining their hands.

(13) SIMONIDES. [. . .] Therefore, hear you, mistress: either frame
      Your will to mine—and you, sir, hear you:
      Either be ruled by me—or I'll make you
      Man and wife.
      Nay, come, **your hands and lips must seal it too**. (*Per*. 2.5.83–7)

(b) Celebration
The love between Ferdinand and Miranda confirmed by their hands in example 12 is further celebrated by hands. In the last act of *The Tempest*, Alonso, the father of Ferdinand, learns of their relationship and probably

36

joins the hands of the couple and himself together in rejoicing their union.

(14) ALONSO. [*to Ferdinand and Miranda*] **Give me your
   hands.**
   Let grief and sorrow still embrace his heart
   That doth not wish you joy! (*Tem.* 5.1.255–8)

(c) Reconciliation and Cooperation

This group contains the largest amount of examples treated in this section. In the first example from *Pericles*, Helicanus is entreated to become King of Tyre by other lords after the long absence of Pericles, but he declines the request and proposes waiting another year for Pericles' return. They agree and hold hands together.

(15) HELICANUS. Then you love us, we you, and **we'll clasp hands.**
   When peers thus knit, a kingdom ever stands. (*Per.* 2.4.59–60)

The following two examples make a pair. Ariel in *The Tempest* plays a trick on Stephano and Trinculo, with the result that they misunderstand each other and quarrel. After a while, they calm down and reconcile, presumably joining their hands. In addition, this repetition of the similar process serves to contribute some humor to the scene.

(16) STEPHANO. **Give me thy hand.** I am sorry I beat thee.
   But while thou liv'st, keep a good tongue in thy
   head. (*Tem.* 3.2.121–3)

(17) STEPHANO. **Give me thy hand.** I do begin to have bloody
   thoughts. (*Tem.* 4.1.245–6)

   In contrast, the examples below do not necessarily imply specific gestures of hands by the characters spoken to, but some movements of hands are naturally involved while they are helping the speakers, Cerimon and Prospero, in the actual performance.

(18) CERIMON. Hush, my gentle neighbors!
  Lend me your hands. To the next chamber bear her.
  Get linen. Now this matter must be looked to,
  For her relapse is mortal. (*Per.* 3.2.124–7)

(19) PROSPERO.   'Tis time
  I should inform thee farther. **Lend thy hand**
  And pluck my magic garment from me. (*Tem.* 1.2.27–9)

(d) Political Courtesy
In the final example below, Lucius, a Roman general, asks for Cloten's
hand before leaving Britain, a request to which Cloten complies. In the
preceding scenes, the failed negotiations between Britain and Rome
prompt Cloten to say that this is the last opportunity to see one another in
an atmosphere of friendship.

(20) LUCIUS. [*to Cloten*]   **Your hand, my lord**.
  CLOTEN. **Receive it friendly**, but from this time forth
    I wear it as your enemy.
  LUCIUS.   Sir, the event
    Is yet to name the winner. Fare you well. (*Cym.* 3.5.16–20)

To summarize, the range of gestures using hands is rather narrow as far
as those instances with explicit references to hands are concerned. Most
of the examples suggest joining hands. This stands in stark contrast to the
wide variety of gestures presented in John Bulwer's *Chirologia* and
Chironomia, published in 1644. Although there is a difference of 36 years
between the year of publication of Bulwer's works and the estimated first
performance date of *Pericles* (1608), it is noteworthy that the types of
hand gestures illustrated or indicated in the lines of the romance plays are
limited. However, we should also note that similar hand gestures are used
with different connotations as observed above. Therefore, it can be argued
that the capacity of hand gestures is not fully documented in the text of
the plays, but the actions with hands have a certain significance in
displaying several types of human relationships.

5. Final Remarks

These observations on the use of 'hand(s)' reveal some characteristics of Shakespeare's romance plays. From the analysis of the adjectives that appear immediately before 'hand(s),' the tendency toward the metonymical use of hands becomes visible. In other words, hands are often regarded as a symbol of the character's personality. Furthermore, the examination of gestures with specific references to hands suggests that only limited kinds of gestures are inferred from the text, but differ in connotation according to the context in which they appear. In order to clarify the characteristics of the use of hand(s) in Shakespeare's plays, we need to analyze the examples found in other genres of plays. Further investigation into the use of adjectives that show up in other positions before and after the word 'hand(s)' and the gestures suggested without reference to hands is also needed.

References

Anthony, Laurence. 2014. AntConc (Version 3.4.4) [Computer Software]. Tokyo: Waseda University. Available from <http://www.laurenceanthony.net/>.

Bartlett, John. 1894. *A complete concordance or verbal index to words, phrases and passages in the dramatic works of Shakespeare*. Reprint, London: Macmillan & Company. 1956.

Bulwer, John. 1644. *Chirologia*. Reprint, New York: AMS Press, 1975.

_____. 1644. *Chironomia*. Reprint, New York: AMS Press, 1975.

Clarke, Mary Cowden. 1843. *The complete concordance to Shakespeare*. Reprint, Cambridge: Cambridge University Press. 2013.

Folger Shakespeare Library. [n.d.] *Shakespeare's plays, sonnets and poems* from Folger digital texts. Retrieved from <www.folgerdigitaltexts.org>.

Harbage, Alfred. 1989. *Annals of English drama 975–1700*. 3rd ed. London: Routledge.

Karim-Cooper, Farah. 2016. *The hand on the Shakespearean stage: gesture, touch and the spectacle of dismemberment*. London: Bloomsbury.

Littlemore, Jeannette. 2015. *Metonymy: hidden shortcuts in language, thought and communication*. Cambridge: Cambridge University Press.

Seto, Ken-ichi. 1999. Distinguishing metonymy from synecdoche. In Klaus-Uwe Panther & Günter Radden (eds.), *Metonymy in language and thought*, 91–120. Amsterdam: John Benjamins Publishing Company.

Northwestern University. 2004–13. WordHoard [Computer Software]. Available from <http://wordhoard.northwestern.edu/userman/index.html>.

Spevack, Marvin. 1968–80. *A complete and systematic concordance to the works of Shakespeare*. 9 vols. Hildesheim: Georg Olms.

_____. 1973. *The Harvard concordance to Shakespeare*. Hildesheim: Georg Olms.

From Convention to Creation: Blushing in Jane Austen with Reference to her Predecessors

Yuko Ikeda

1. Introduction

In the novels of Jane Austen (1775–1817), characters' facial expression often uncovers their emotional state and interpersonal relationships more faithfully than verbal communication. 'Women were thought to express emotions with their bodies more sincerely and spontaneously than men;' as Todd (1986:19) claims, 'hence their propensity to crying, blushing and fainting.'[1] Acts of blushing, in particular, are characterized as 'automatic reactions' (Korte 1997: 65), with these involuntary responses revealing the delicate female feeling linked to the cult of sensibility[2] as seen in Gothic and sentimental novels in the latter half of the eighteenth century.

It might be worth noting the social implication of blushing before starting a particular discussion about its use. The act of blushing is closely

---

[1] Mullan (1988: 201) similarly argues that 'exceptional virtue' or 'intensified forms of communication' is connoted by tears, blushes and sighs.

[2] The mid-eighteenth century, especially from the 1740s to the 1770s, is generally known as the age of sensibility. As for blushing and sensibility, see McMaster (2004), Mullan (1988) and Gorman (1993). Korte (1997: 130) asserts that during this period 'body language became a favoured and often the only means to convey emotional states' because speech was 'no longer considered sufficient to express feelings.' This paper focuses on women's propensity to blush particularly with reference to their sensibility and other hidden feelings, though men also blush occasionally.

related to the cultivation of feminine women with sensibility, which was promoted in a proliferation of conduct books, which acted as moral guidelines for young women in the eighteenth century. John Gregory, for example, in his *Father's Legacy to His Daughters* (1774), one of the most popular conduct books, recommends that females blush as a sign of sensibility. Blushing is considered as an attractive attribute of women which imparts a glow to their cheeks with the flow of blood and improves their countenance. Gregory states that '[w]hen a girl ceases to blush, she has lost the most powerful charm of beauty. [. . .] Blushing is so far from being necessarily an attendant on guilt, that it is the usual companion of innocence' (Gregory 1996: 15–16).

Inheriting the eighteenth-century conventional meaning of blush as 'a cultural sign' (Wiltshire 1992: 77) of sensibility connected to female modesty and innocence, Austen seems to add some creative use to this body language in a way which interacts with the overall structure and the theme of the works.[3] Among the previous studies about Austen's body language is McMaster's *Reading the Body in the Eighteenth-Century Novel*, which is mainly concerned with 'reading the mind through the body' (McMaster 2004: x) in the novels of the eighteenth century. In the last chapter of her overall research, entitled 'Epilogue: And On To Jane Austen,' McMaster suggests that Austen, though sharing with her prede-cessors, is distinguished with her 'selection and understatement' (McMaster 2004: 174) in the use of body language. The extensive exploration of Wiltshire (1992) and Gorman (1993) also gives us insight into Austen's novels in the light of body, health and illness. Gorman regards 'blushing' and 'blanching' as the index of emotion, while Wiltshire reads modesty and sensitivity into Fanny Price's blushing. J. O'Farrell (1997), centering her observation on the argument of complexions in nineteenth-century novels, explains the use of the blush in *Pride and Prejudice*. Taking these studies into consideration, the main interest in the present paper is to examine Austen's use of blushing in the chronological context from the mid eighteenth to the early nineteenth century, from Richardson to Austen,

---

[3] By the 1790s, when Austen started to write novels, the term sensibility had already come to possess a pejorative meaning connected with excessive emotion and a lack of reason.

in order to explore how the author makes her way from convention to creation.[4]

My first area of investigation concerns the use of blushing in the novels which greatly impacted Austen. I deal with several novels from the eighteenth century to the turn of the century to examine the general shift in the usage of blushing: from Richardson's *Pamela* (1740) and *Clarissa* (1748), to five novels by female authors: Fanny Burney's *Evelina* (1778), followed by an examination of Charlotte Smith's *Emmeline* (1788), Elizabeth Inchbald's *A Simple Story* (1791), Ann Radcliffe's *The Mysteries of Udolpho* (1794), and Maria Edgeworth's *Belinda* (1801).

Next, I turn to the problem of how Austen takes over and modifies the conventional use of blushing represented by her predecessors. The final section focuses on a thorough analysis of Jane Fairfax's blushing in *Emma,* which functions not only as a sign of emotional states and interpersonal relationships, but also as a signal to uncover the hidden message and the thematic strategy of the novel.

2. Blushing in Samuel Richardson

It is well known that Richardson had a great impact on Austen, especially in the representation of characters' emotions. This section aims to clarify some distinctive uses of blushing in Richardson's *Pamela* and *Clarissa*. The term blush has been used as an important signal to represent female sensibility as McMaster (2004: 103) asserts in analyzing *Clarissa*: 'The faltering tongue, the downcast eye, the sigh, and the give-away blush, are signs spontaneous and reliable, and not to be counterfeited.' Moreover, according to Korte (1997: 184), '[i]t is with Richardson that a novel tradition begins to emerge in which the expressive potential of body language can be exploited to the full.'

2.1. The Blush of sensibility

First, let us examine Richardson's use of the word blush in representing

---

[4] I limit this study exclusively to the use of 'blush' for clarification, thus excluding other expressions indicative of a change of color. My major interest in this paper is the qualitative examination in the use of blushing rather than quantitative analysis. Italics in quotations are all mine unless otherwise indicated.

44

female sensibility. One of characteristic structures is the collocation of 'blush' linked to other words by the use of 'and':

(1) So, like a fool, I was ready to cry; and went away *curcheeing and blushing*, I am sure, up to the Ears; for, tho' there was no Harm in what he said, yet I did not know how to take it. (*Pamela* 19)

(2) What could he mean by letting slip such a one as that you mention?—I don't know how to blame you neither. How could you go beyond *silence and blushes*, when the foolish fellow came with his observances of the restrictions which you laid him under when in another situation? (*Clarissa* 432)

(3) She saw me *hesitate and blush*, and said, Well, you know best; but. . . . (*Pamela* 323)

(4) . . . full of *blushes and pretty confusion*, might be supposed to express. . . . (*Clarissa* 539)

(5) . . . by your Eyes, *your Blushes, and that sweet Confusion* which I behold struggling in your Bosom, ... (*Pamela* 213)

In quotations (1) and (2), blushing is linked to 'curchee'('courtesy') and 'silence,' which indicates that both heroines blush in place of uttering actual words. In (3), blushing is a sign of female hesitation before starting verbal communication; in the examples (4) and (5), the act of blushing is combined with 'confusion' which is modified by 'pretty' and 'sweet' respectively. This collocation suggests a male perspective which interprets female blushing as pretty or showing sweet confusion. Though neither heroine articulates what they feel with their speech, the male characters try to read their emotions, such as embarrassment and confusion, through their blushing.

2.2. Blushing under a piercing male gaze

It is often the case that female characters blush under the watchful eye of male characters who regard the female blush as a charming sign of sensibility as seen in the passages below:

(6) None of your *Considerings!* said he, Pretty-face, and tapp'd me on the Cheek. I blush'd, but was glad he was so good-humour'd; . . . . (*Pamela* 211) (Italics original)

(7) Don't blush, *Pamela*, said he—As his back was to me, I thought I would speak to the Man, and before he saw me, I said, How do you, old Acquaintance? (for, said he, you know we were of one College for a twelvemonth.) (*Pamela* 281) (Italics original)

(8) 'Blush, then, delicacy! that cannot bear the poet's *Amor omnibus idem!*—Blush, then, purity!' (*Clarissa* 223) (Italics original)

(9) '—I will say, Sir, said I, and hid my blushing Face on his Bosom, that your Wishes, in every thing, shall be mine; but, pray, Sir, say no more!' (*Pamela* 374)

In *Pamela*, as seen in quotations (6) and (7), the master decodes confusion in Pamela's blush, which involuntarily discloses her inner state of mind. In example (9), Pamela hides her face from his piercing eye for fear that her master, seeing her blush, reads her inner feelings.

As examined above, in Richardson's novels, the female blush is regarded as a sign of sensibility representing modesty and reserve as well as such feelings as embarrassment, confusion, gratitude, and shame. These interpretations are mainly from the male perspective, because in many situations, the female body is exposed to the fixed gaze of men, as an object to be watched.

3. Women writers' use of blushing

This section deals with the novels of female writers in the late eighteenth and the early nineteenth centuries, a period distinguished by an increase in the number of female authors. The five novels I discuss here, which deeply affected Austen, have something in common in their representation of the blushing of female figures, though they may differ to some extent in the way and the focus of attention.[5]

---

[5] Most are generally referred to as courtship novels or sentimental (gothic) novels

46

3.1. The blush of sensibility

As in the case of Richardson's novels, female writers often employ blushing to convey a sign of female sensibility. As seen in the excerpts (10) to (15), blushing is connected with such words as 'tremble,' 'hesitate,' 'thoughtful,' 'silent' and 'smile,' especially in *Udolpho* and *Emmeline*:

(10) . . . while Emmeline, *trembling and blushing*, endeavoured to recollect herself, and said—. . . . (*Emmeline* 18)

(11) 'God forbid it ever should!' said Emmeline, with quickness: 'for then,' continued she, *hesitating and blushing*, ... (*Emmeline* 282)

(12) . . . She *blushed, and became thoughtful*. (*Udoplho* 10)

(13) Emily *blushed, and was silent*. . . . (*Udolpho* 210)

(14) Emily *blushed and smiled*, and Madame Cheron spared her the difficulty of replying. (*Udolpho* 132)

(15) Godolphin, however, was still pressing; and at length brought her to confess, with *blushes and even with tears*, her early and long partiality for him, ... (*Emmeline* 404)

One of the characteristic uses of these female writers differing from those of Richardson can be found in their visual expressions of blushing, which stand out in sharp contrast to the pale complexion of female figures. The change of color caused by blushing is so conspicuous that it is difficult for them to keep others from reading their emotions:

(16) . . . and *blushed* over *her pallid countenance*. . . . (*A Simple Story* 97–8)

(17) . . . *deep blushes dyed* the cheeks of the *fair* orphan. . . . (*Emmeline* 396)

---

with young women's development of mind at the center. Inchbald's *A Simple Story*, however, may be categorized as a 'Jacobin' novel with a feminist implication. See also the introduction of *A Simple Story* (1998: vii–xx).

(18) On entering the room, through all *the dead white of her present complexion, she blushed to a crimson. (A Simple Story* 189)

(19) When Lady Delacour pulled off Belinda's mask, her face was during the first instant, *pale; the next moment, crimsoned over with a burning blush.* (*Belinda* 27)

(20) Emmeline, whose *colourless cheeks were suffused with a deep blush* at this speech, hastily interrupted it.— (*Emmeline* 354)

The word blush is frequently modified by the adverb 'deeply,' or the adjectives 'deep' and 'burning.' There are also such expressions as 'deep blushes dyed' and 'a crimson.' Interestingly, their blushed faces are visually highlighted against a pale complexion, as illustrated by such words as 'pallid,' 'fair,' 'dead white,' 'pale,' and 'colourless.'

3.2. Blushing linked with various emotions

In addition to the direct collocation with the use of 'and,' there are also some cases in which a blush is contextually linked to such words revealing various character emotions, including shame, gratitude and confusion as seen below:

(21) [. . .] 'mark but her *blushing cheek!*'
'And then her eye,—*her downcast eye!*' cried another. (*Evelina 326*)

(22) . . . her *gratitude* was expressed in *blushes,* . . . . (*A Simple Story* 134)

(23) . . . if Belinda *blushed,* it was merely from the *confusion* into which she was thrown by the piercing glance of Lady Delacour's black eyes. . . . (*Belinda* 185)

There is also the case in which blushing is accompanied by verbal utterances of disagreement:

(24)   'Good God!' *exclaimed* Emily, *blushing deeply,* 'it is surely impossible my aunt could thus have represented me!' (*Udolpho* 286)

48

(25) After dinner Lady Delacour, having made Belinda *protest and blush, and blush and protest*, that her head was not running upon the twisted note, began the history of her life and opinions in the following manner: . . . . (*Belinda* 35)

In both quotations (24) and (25), the heroines blush when they are made fun of with regard to their favor towards the male figures. While they dare not give voice to their thoughts or contradict the opinions of authoritative persons, blushing reveals their inner emotions.

3.3. Ambiguous blushing

Female characters' acts of blushing are sometimes difficult to interpret. For example, it is on occasion unclear as to whether blushing is a sign of modesty or a result of female consciousness of improper feelings:

(26) 'Mere play upon words! words! All shame is false shame. We should be a great deal better without it. What say you, Miss Portman? Silent—hey? Silence that speaks!'
  'Miss Portman's blushes,' said Mr. Vincent, 'speak *for her.*'
  '*Against* her,' said Mrs. Freke. 'Women blush because they understand.'
  'And you would have them understand without blushing?' said Mr. Percival.
  'So would I; for nothing can be more different than innocence and ignorance. Female delicacy—' (*Belinda* 229) (Italics original)

As for the decoding of women's blushing, there remains some ambiguity as to how it should be interpreted. In the quotation above,[6] it is debatable whether acts of remaining silent and blushing speak 'for' or 'against' Belinda, because blushing involuntary reveals what she hides, namely her affection for the man. Accordingly, the argument about what her blushing implies suggests that it can be interpreted not only as a sign of women's modesty, but also as a sign of improper feelings or sexual consciousness: 'women blush because they understand.'

---

[6] Wiltshire (1992: 82) claims that '[b]lushing resembles a hysterical symptom in that its communication is ambiguous.'

The following passage from *A Simple Story* demonstrates the further difficulty in decoding this non-verbal signal:

(27) 'I shall,' answered she, 'and not consent to marry a man whom I could never love.'

'Unless your heart is already given away, Miss Milner, what can make you speak with such a degree of certainty?'

He thought on Lord Frederick while he said this, and he fixed his eyes upon her as if he wished to penetrate her sentiments, and yet trembled for what he might find there.—*She blushed, and her looks would have confirmed her guilty, had not a free and unembarrassed tone of voice, more than her words, preserved her from that sentence.*

'No,' she replied, 'my heart is not given away, and yet I can venture to declare Sir Edward will never possess an atom of it.' (*A Simple Story* 25)

Dorriforth interprets Miss Miller's blushing as a clear sign of affirmation in regards to his assumption that she declined Sir Edward's marriage offer because her mind was preoccupied with Lord Frederick. However, his interpretation was disproved by the succeeding sentence with 'a free and unembarrassed tone of voice.' The interpretation of blushing is rather complicated and deeply incorporated into the broader narrative context which discloses that Miss Miller is passionately in love with Dorriforth himself.

As has been examined above, usage of the female blush in the late eighteenth-century novels primarily illustrates women's sensibility. However, it can be seen that expressions related to blushing become more diversified and visually specified compared to the use of abstract words in Richardson. Moreover, a variety of feelings are imparted with female blushing, including sensibility, shame, gratitude, confusion, and protest. There is also the case in which female blushing is ambiguously utilized as either a sign of innocence or as an awareness of improper feelings.

4. Creative use of blushing in Jane Austen

As has been examined in the previous sections, blushing is often used conventionally as a device through which to reveal women's delicate sensibility, bearing similarities to the use of shyness, modesty and

50

quietness. In Richardson's novels, an involuntary manifestation of inner self also underlines women's embarrassment under the gaze of men. For various female writers in the late eighteenth century, blushing increasingly implies women's complicated and ambiguous feelings, as well as a sign of sensibility. Let us examine how Austen inherits the conventional use, skillfully adding her originality in ways that both mirror and differ from her predecessors.[7]

4.1. The blush of sensibility as parody
Rather than following the conventional use of blushing to denote female sensibility, Austen distinguishes herself in taking advantage of its use for parody:

(28) . . . but Mr. Tilney, within three yards of the place where they sat; he seemed to be moving that way, but *he did not see her, and therefore the smile and the blush*, which his sudden reappearance raised in Catherine, passed away without sullying *her heroic importance*. (*NA* 48)[8]

In *Northanger Abbey*, the novel known as a parody of Radcliffe's *Udolpho,* blushing is employed rather as a mockery of sentimental novels in which the hero is attracted to a beautiful heroine who responds to him with 'the smile and the blush.' Austen seems to make use of this set phrase so as to ridicule the convention by reversing the process: it was Catherine who blushed and smiled first in encountering the man she feels attachment with, and as Henry did not even see her face, Catherine's blush and smile passed unnoticed 'without sullying *her heroic importance*.' The narrator's ironic tone is evident.[9]

---

[7] As for the study of Austen's blushing, see Gorman (1993) and Wiltshire (1992). Gorman argues that Austen's use of blushing is 'less sentimental and more suggestive' compared to her predecessors (Gorman 128).

[8] The following abbreviation is used: *Sense and Sensibility (SS), Pride and Prejudice (PP), Mansfield Park (MP), Emma (E), Northanger Abbey (NA).*

[9] It is important to take the social code into account, where a woman should not reveal her affection to a man before it is shown to her by him, as seen in Gregory's maxim that 'love is not to begin on your part, but is entirely to be the consequence of our attachment to you' (Gregory 1996: 36).

Austen also uses the stock phrase of 'blush and smile' for the characterization of Harriet Smith in *Emma*, a gentle and submissive marginal figure:

(29) . . . and Harriet *blushed and smiled*, and said she had always thought Mr. Elton very agreeable. (*E* 34) / Harriet *blushed and smiled*, and said something about wondering that people should like her so much. (*E* 58)

There are also examples of the fixed phrase of '*blushing as she spoke*' in parenthesis as shown below:

(30) '. . . what I ought never to have kept—I know that very well (*blushing as she spoke*). . . .' said she, with a conscious look. (*E* 366) / 'Had you any idea,' cried Harriet, 'of his being in love with her?—You, perhaps, might. You (*blushing as she spoke*) who can see into everybody's heart; but nobody else—' (*E* 441)

Such conventional collocations as 'blushed and smiled' and 'blushing as she spoke' are employed as a mechanical fixed pattern. The author's mocking attitude might be assumed by her consistent choice of these expressions not for heroines, but for a minor character such as Harriet.

4.2. The blush of mixed feelings

Instead of the conventional collocation of 'blush and smile,' there is the combination of 'blush and laugh' for the heroine Emma:

(31) She stopt to *blush and laugh at* her own relapse, and then resumed a more serious, more dispiriting cogitation upon what had been, and might be, and must be. (*E* 148)

(32) Emma recollected, *blushed, was sorry, but tried to laugh it off.*
'Nay, how could I help saying what I did?—Nobody could have helped it. It was not so very bad. I dare say she did not understand me.' (*E* 407)

(33)   'Impossible!—I never can call you any thing but 'Mr. Knightley.' I will not promise even to equal the elegant terseness of Mrs. Elton, by calling you Mr. K.—But I will promise,' she added presently, *laughing and blushing*—'I will promise to call you once by your Christian name. . . .' (*E* 505)

52

It is significant to note the different implication of 'laugh' and 'smile.' In eighteenth-century conduct writings, the act of laughing by women is warned against as it was considered to be subversive and dangerous to stability.[10] Blushing in the quotations (31) and (32) indicate Emma's reflection on her conduct and errors, though it is at the same time linked to the more assertive 'laugh' rather than the more conventional and milder 'smile.' The passage in (33) illustrates Emma's response to Mr. Knightley's request to call him something other than 'Mr. Knightley' after marriage. Emma promises to call him by his Christian name, which makes her blush and laugh. It would appear that Emma laughs in order to hide her embarrassment. A similar combination of 'blush' and 'laugh,' implying the heroine's mixed feelings, is also seen in *Evelina*.[11]

4.3. The blush of protest and indignation

In Austen's novels, blushing is sometimes deeply associated with women's protest and indignation in contexts where they cannot openly articulate their thoughts and opinions due to modesty and social restriction.

Mansfield Park's Fanny, the least lively of all her heroines, is a quiet listener, and her propensity to blush relates to her quiet disposition. Fanny blushes when she dares to speak her own opinion or to contradict others:

(34) She had never spoken so much at once to him in her life before, and never so angrily to any one; and when her speech was over, she *trembled and blushed* at her own daring. (*MP* 263)

(35) *With the deepest blushes Fanny protested* against such a thought.
'Well then,' replied Miss Crawford more seriously but without at all believing her, 'to convince me that you suspect no trick, and are as unsuspicious of compliment as I have always found you, take the necklace, and say no more about it. . . .' (*MP* 301–2)

---

[10] Audrey Bilger, for instance, states that 'laughter's impolite qualities set it at odds with the norms of eighteenth-century manners' (Bilger 1998:16).

[11] 'I interrupted him—*I blush for my folly,—with laughing*; yet I could not help it; for, added to the man's stately foppishness, . . . when I looked around at Lord Orville, I saw such extreme surprise in his face,—the cause of which appeared so absurd, that I could not for my life preserve my gravity' (*Evelina* 34).

Though Fanny is generally timid, shy, and quiet, she never changes her opinion when she believes it is right. It seems that Fanny's verbal communication accompanied with blushing implies her confliction between mildness and firmness of mind. Blushing may even reveal that she is caught in a double bind between her anger, and the consciousness that such behavior digresses from the conventional social code that requires women to be modest, gentle and submissive.

In the following examples, blushing is an emblem of stronger feelings, such as shame and vexation:

(36) When Mr. Collins said anything of which his wife might reasonably be ashamed, which certainly was not unseldom,[12] she involuntarily turned her eye on Charlotte. Once or twice *she could discern a faint blush*; but in general Charlotte wisely did not hear. (*PP* 177)

(37)   Nothing that she could say, however, had any influence. Her mother would talk of her views in the same intelligible tone. Elizabeth *blushed and blushed again with shame and vexation*. (*PP* 111–12)

(38)   'Indeed, Mama, you are mistaken,' said Elizabeth, *blushing for her mother*. 'You quite mistook Mr. Darcy. He only meant that there were not such a variety of people to be met with in the country as in the town, which you must acknowledge to be true.' (*PP* 47)

(39) Elizabeth had not before believed him quite equal to such assurance; but she sat down, resolving within herself, to draw no limits in future to the impudence of an impudent man. *She* blushed, and Jane blushed; but the cheeks of the two who caused their confusion suffered no variation of colour. (*PP* 349) (Italics original)

(40)   *Elinor blushed for the insincerity of Edward's future wife*, and replied, 'this compliment would effectually frighten me from giving any opinion on the subject had I formed one. It raises my influence much too high; the power of dividing two people so tenderly attached is too much for an indifferent person.' (*SS* 171)

---

[12] The Cambridge edition gives a note for 'not unseldom' as a misuse for 'not rarely, not frequently' (*PP* 498).

54

'A faint blush' discerned by Elizabeth's observation of her friend's complexion in example (36) suggests Charlotte's shame for her husband, while (37) and (38) suggests Elizabeth's shame for her mother. Example (39) represents Elizabeth and Jane's anger at Wickham, and (40) reveals Elinor's indignation for the insincerity of Lucy. In all cases, blushing, in place of verbal language, can be interpreted as a spontaneous manifestation of their shame and anger rather than as the representation of their sensibility.

4.4. The self-conscious blush

In Austen's novels, there are some cases in which a character is conscious of her own blush as seen in the following passage. When Elizabeth talks about the distance from her parents' house after marriage, Darcy momentarily misunderstands her blush as a sign of her favor for him, though Elizabeth blushes because, as she assumes, he knows she is talking of Bingley and Jane:

(41) As he spoke there was a sort of smile which Elizabeth fancied she understood; he must be supposing her to be thinking of Jane and Netherfield, and she blushed as she answered, ...

Mr. Darcy drew his chair a little towards her, and said, '*You* cannot have a right to such very strong local attachment. *You* cannot have been always at Longbourn.'

Elizabeth looked surprised. The gentleman experienced some change of feeling; he drew back his chair, took a newspaper from the table, and, glancing over it, said, in a colder voice,

'Are you pleased with Kent?' (*PP* 201) (Italics original)

This is the scene in which the blush functions as a trigger for other body language. Darcy's misinterpretation of Elizabeth's blush as her affection toward him and his later awareness of his misreading is represented by the control of distance between them: 'drew his chair a little towards her' and 'drew back his chair, took a newspaper from the table,' which Korte categorizes as 'Proxemics' (Korte 1997: 73–8). It is assumed that misinterpretation of blushing plays a crucial role in the dramatization of their interpersonal relationship and different emotional states in a larger context: Darcy is attached to Elizabeth, while she is not aware of his affection.[13]

Similarly, in the passage from *Northanger Abbey*, a woman's consciousness of her blush is brought into focus mockingly:

(42) 'It is very true, however; you shall read James's letter yourself. — Stay—there is one part—' *recollecting with a blush the last line.*
'Will you take the trouble of reading to us the passages which concern my brother?'
'No, read it yourself,' cried Catherine, whose second thoughts were clearer. 'I do not know what I was thinking of,' (*blushing again that she had blushed before*). . . . (*NA* 210)

So far I have demonstrated some distinctive features in Austen's use of blushing. Austen's works are written to take advantage of and even ridicule convention, rather than to represent sensibility. The diversity of emotions imparted in blushing, such as shame, indignation and protest, enhances difficulties in interpretation, which may be shared to a degree with some of the eighteenth-century women writers examined above. However, it seems that Austen is interested in putting this ambiguity to use contextually for characterization and in describing interpersonal relationships.

5. Jane Fairfax's blush in *Emma*

The previous section suggests how Austen modifies her use of blushing rather than following in the footsteps of her predecessors. Lastly, I give a detailed analysis of Jane Fairfax's blushing in *Emma* with regard to the thematic strategy of the novel as a whole.

There are two things to take into account in examining the use of Jane's blushing. First, in place of verbal communication, her blushing functions

---

[13] As for Austen's dramatic application of blushing, refer to Wiltshire: 'The blush is not a straightforward phenomenon of the body, rather one of the acutest signs of the bodily enigma, and its deployment in Austen's narratives is governed by her awareness of its problematic nature, and of the possibility of exploiting this for dramatic purposes' (Wiltshire 1992: 18).

56

as a secret language. Reserved and mysterious, Jane rarely speaks her opinion openly, but her occasional blushing discloses her hidden emotions as well as her interpersonal relationships. Interestingly, Jane's fair complexion is often talked about: Frank caustically remarks on her 'most deplorable want of complexion' (*E* 214), to which Emma opposingly states that 'a softness and delicacy in her skin' gives 'peculiar elegance to the character of her face' (*E* 214).[14]

Second, the problem of perspective is also crucial in decoding this body language in *Emma,* which in most cases takes Emma's viewpoint, though the story is narrated through a third person. From the beginning of the story, however, we are shown how Emma makes a series of blunders. At the end of Book I of the novel, by the time Frank and Jane are introduced to the story, we should have some suspicion regarding Emma's interpretation of events. These doubts in mind, the reader is forced to decode Jane's blushing through Emma's eyes. Therefore, we may presume that depending on Emma for interpretation necessarily involves some misconceptions.

5.1. Jane's blush and Emma's misinterpretation
Reserved and mysterious, Jane rarely speaks her opinion openly, but often blushes, and not without reason. Let us first examine what is in Jane's blushes with reference to the structure of the novel. With a keen interest in Jane, Emma constantly keeps a close eye on her to interpret her feelings through her facial expressions and, in particular, through her blushing. The first example occurs when Jane gets the anonymous gift of a piano:

(43)   In so large a party it was not necessary that Emma should approach her. . . .
she saw *the blush of consciousness* with which congratulations were received, *the blush of guilt* which accompanied the name of 'my excellent friend Col. Campbell.' (*E* 237)

---

[14] Mrs. Elton compares Jane with a flower 'born to blush unseen' (*E* 305), wondering if Jane's beauty and talents remain unknown to the world because of her situation as an orphan, quoting Thomas Gray's 'Elegy Written in a Country Churchyard'(lines 55).

Emma 'saw the blush of consciousness' on Jane's face as a sign that she is consciously hiding something, in addition to 'the blush of guilt' when she mentions the name of Col. Campbell. Somehow, Emma suspects Mr. Dixon as the sender of the piano, and connects this body language with Jane's improper relationship with the married man.

Similarly, in the next scene, we see Jane's deep blush in response to Frank's praise of Col. Campbell as very thoughtful:

(44)   'Here is something quite new to me. Do you know it?—Cramer. And here are a new set of Irish melodies. . . . . Very thoughtful of Col. Campbell, was not it?—He knew Miss Fairfax could have no music here. . . . . True affection only could have prompted it.'

Emma wished he would be less pointed, yet could not help being amused; and when on glancing her eye towards Jane Fairfax she caught the remains of a smile, when she saw that with *all the deep blush of consciousness*, there had been *a smile of secret delight*, ... (*E* 262)

Emma, as a keen observer of the scene, takes Jane's 'all the deep blush of consciousness' to mean that it reveals her confusion resulting from Frank's allusion to the affection of the sender, most probably Mr. Dixon. Though we read the story according to Emma's interpretation, we feel something is wrong about her conclusion. When we connect a variety of hidden hints in the narrative with Frank's behavior and Jane's blush, we gradually develop a different interpretation: there is some secret relationship between Frank and Jane, and Frank makes use of Emma's misinterpretation. If we reread Jane's blushing as relating to the sender of the piano, we may conjecture that Jane blushes because she knows the real sender of the piano, Frank, and she wants to hide their secret relationship. Emma is right in tracing something immoral in Jane's blush, but her biased view clouds her judgement.

This is secret communication, and Jane's blush is a silent signal involuntarily revealing her complex inner state of embarrassment. Conscious of their secret relationship, she suffers from a sense of guilt, in addition to anger at Frank's insensibility. Reading to this point, we are able to gain a different interpretation of Jane's blushing from Emma, and guess the hidden message.

58

In the next example, Jane walks to the post office in the rain to get a letter. Mr. John Knightley worries about her catching cold in the rain, while Jane is unusually assertive in getting her letter by herself with a blush and tears:

(45)　'[. . .] Miss Fairfax, that ten years hence you may have as many concentrated objects as I have.'

It was kindly said, and very far from giving offence. A pleasant 'thank you' seemed meant *to laugh it off, but a blush, a quivering lip, a tear in the eye, shewed that it was felt beyond a laugh.* (*E* 317–18)

Emma concludes, after watching and listening carefully, that a glow on Jane's face is a sign of happiness from receiving a letter from someone she loves, perhaps Mr. Dixon. This time the clue that this interpretation may not be accurate is proffered by Frank's father, Mr. Weston, who arrives just after this scene with a letter from Frank saying that he is visiting Highbury soon. We assume that the letter Jane received is also from Frank, not from Dixon. That may be the reason for her unusual glow. Emma's interpretation is close, but again misses the mark due to her fixed notion concerning Dixon.

As shown above, Jane's blushing can be better explained in a larger context: not only by Emma's reading, but also with Frank's verbal and non-verbal communication, and with contextual clues throughout the novel.[15] If we take Frank's mysterious impatience and restlessness into consideration, as seen in such body language as his moving immediately, going to the door, watching for the carriages, and staring at Jane, we can discover that all are connected to his affection for Jane. In this context Jane's blushing makes perfect sense.

5.2. Jane's blushing and Mr. Knightley's interpretation

At this stage of the novel, we are becoming more and more doubtful of

---

[15] Frank's behavior is often enigmatic to Emma, and even to the reader at the first reading. This is the result of Austen's particular strategy: we are distracted and cheated by Frank's deliberate schemes, such as his finding fault with Jane, his flirtation with Emma, and his making use of Emma's fantasy about Mr. Dixon.

Emma's interpretation, and more suspicious of the relationship between Frank and Jane. This can be justified by the introduction of another perspective, Mr. Knightley's, who in place of Emma plays the role of clarifying our doubt by solving contradictions and explaining the true message of Jane's blushing. Knightley is ever conscious of Emma's behavior, including how she behaves among other people. Somehow, he notices Frank's glances at Jane, and justifies us in our doubt about their intimate relationship. Let us consider the following scene in which the story is narrated through Mr. Knightley's perspective:

(46) Frank was next to Emma, Jane opposite to them—and Mr. Knightley so placed as to see them all; and it was his object to see as much as he could, with as little apparent observation. The word was discovered, and with a faint smile pushed away. . . . The word was *blunder*; and as Harriet exultingly proclaimed it, there was a blush on Jane's cheek which gave it a meaning not otherwise ostensible. Mr. Knightley connected it with the dream; but how it could all be, was beyond his comprehension. (*E* 377) (Italics original)

Frank makes use of a children's word game to give the secret message to Jane. Knightley observes both the first card 'blunder' and Jane's blushing in reaction. Her blush 'gave it a meaning not otherwise ostensible.' He connects it with 'dream,' though the real message is 'beyond his comprehension.' This is the clue for us, because the word 'dream' refers to Frank's speech about 'I am a great dreamer' (*E* 374) as well as Miss Bates's in the preceding situation. Miss Bates wonders why Frank knows about Mr. Perry's plan for having a carriage even though she has not told anyone of it except Jane: 'I am a talker, you know; I am rather a talker . . . I am not like Jane; I wish I were. . . . Extraordinary dream indeed!' (*E* 375–6). If we connect their speech about 'dream' with the card 'blunder,' and Jane's blushing, we can logically reach the conclusion that Jane somehow divulges the information to Frank, maybe through secret correspondence between them. Therefore, by the card 'blunder,' Frank refers to his own blunder of letting slip the information he got from Jane's letter. The message of the card, as well as the blushing, serves as secret language which may not make sense to anyone except them. The second card Frank gives to Jane is 'Dixon':

60

(47) Mr. Knightley's excessive curiosity to know what this word might be, . . . and it was not long before he saw it to be *Dixon*. Jane Fairfax's perception seemed to accompany his; her comprehension was certainly more equal to the covert meaning, the superior intelligence, of those five letters so arranged. She was evidently displeased; looked up, and seeing herself watched, blushed more deeply than he had ever perceived her, and saying only, 'I did not know that proper names were allowed,' pushed away the letters with even an angry spirit, ... (*E* 378) (Italics original)

This time Jane reacts more openly. She 'blushed more deeply than he had ever perceived,' indicating her strong indignation against Frank. Emma thinks Jane is angry because she is mocked for her relationship with Mr. Dixon, while Knightley suggests a different explanation for her anger. Jane's blushing reveals Frank's insincere and immoral character, considering Jane's suffering and moral oppression regarding their secret engagement. Through this word game, the reader is also challenged to decode the signs correctly.

In summary, it is possible to make several observations. First, Jane's blushing is a significant key to uncovering her secret communication with Frank. In situations where verbal communication is limited, her blushing functions as a silent language with a variety of messages, implying the emotional state of characters and their interpersonal relationships, as well as thematic messages. Second, what characterizes this novel is how the use of this body language is concerned with the malfunction of encoding and decoding. Though we begin reading the novel from Emma's perspective, we become increasingly suspicious of her interpretation of events, and at some stage of the novel, we can gain better perspective than Emma with the help of Mr. Knightley's correct reading of the situation. Though Austen gives us numerous, but obscure, hints throughout the novel, it is up to the reader to discern whether the message is correctly decoded or not. Consequently, Austen's use of blushing in *Emma* is neither conservative nor overt but suggestive, in the sense that it leads us to more comprehensive understanding of the structure of the novel.

6. Final Remarks

I have thus far examined Austen's use of blushing in comparison with her predecessors. In Richardson's novels, the use of blushing is mainly concerned with the conventional representation of female sensibility, such as modesty, shyness, embarrassment and confusion. In many situations, the female blush is influenced and interpreted from a male perspective.

One of the distinctive features in the novels of late eighteenth-century female authors is the diversity and particularity of expressions related to the word 'blush.' Blushing may be a signal for female delicate feelings and sensibility, but it also suggests their confusion and protest, including ambiguous feelings. Some cases cast a light on ambiguity in interpretation, where female blushing may be understood as a sign of innocence, or as an awareness of improper feelings.

Austen seems to be more interested in developing the scope and application of this body language so that it can be integrated into a wider context for dramatic purposes, rather than faithfully taking the conventional use of her predecessors as a model. In *Emma,* blushing is one of the key elements to deciphering the relationship between two characters with limited verbal communication, which also makes us aware of the problem of decoding character non-verbal communication based on multiple perspectives in the broader framework of the novel as a whole.

References

Austen, Jane. 2005–6. The Cambridge Edition of the Works of Jane Austen. Cambridge: Cambridge University Press.

Bilger, Audrey. 1998. *Laughing feminism: subversive comedy in Frances Burney, Maria Edgeworth, and Jane Austen.* Detroit: Wayne State University Press.

Burney, Frances. 2002. *Evelina.* Oxford: Oxford University Press.

Edgeworth, Maria. 1999. *Belinda.* Oxford: Oxford University Press.

Gorman, Anita G. 1985. *The body in illness and health: Themes and images in Jane Austen.* New York: Peter Lang.

Jones, Vivien (ed.). 1990. *Women in the eighteenth century.* London: Routledge.

62

Inchbald, Elizabeth. 1998. *A simple story.* Oxford: Oxford University Press.

Korte, Barbara. 1997. *Body language in literature.* Toronto: University of Toronto Press.

McMaster, Juliet. 1991. The secret languages of *Emma. Persuasions* 13, 119–31.

_____. 2004. *Reading the body in the eighteenth-century novel.* Palgrave Macmillan.

Mullan, John. 1988. *Sentiment and sociability: The language of feeling in the eighteenth century.* Oxford: Clarendon Press.

O'Farrell, Mary Ann. 1997. *Telling complexions: The nineteenth-century English novel and the blush.* Durham: Duke University Press.

Radcliffe, Ann. 1979. *The Mysteries of Udolpho.* Oxford: Oxford University Press.

Richardson, Samuel. 2004. *Clarissa.* London: Penguin Books.

_____. 2001. *Pamela.* Oxford: Oxford University Press.

Smith, Charlotte. *Emmeline.* 2005. London: Pickering & Chatto.

Shields, Carol. 1991. Jane Austen images of the body: No fingers, no toes. *Persuasions 13,* 132–7.

Todd, Janet (ed.). 1996. *Female education in the age of enlightenment.* James Fordyce, *Sermons for young women* (1766), John Gregory, *Father's legacy to his daughters* (1774). London: Pickering & Chatto.

_____. *Sensibility.* 1986. *An introduction.* London: Methuen.

Wiltshire, John. 1992. *Jane Austen and the body.* Cambridge: Cambridge University Press.

The Characters' Eyes and Eye Behavior in Gaskell's *Sylvia's Lovers*

Aiko Saiki

1. Introduction

It has been pointed out[1] that Elizabeth Gaskell (1810–65) prefers a detailed description of people and things in her works.[2] Bonaparte (1992: 10) states that 'Gaskell is extremely visual and she depicts in vivid detail whatever she imagines.' In *Sylvia's Lovers* (1863), this partiality for detail is conspicuous in her illustration of characters' physical appearances, in particular, her diversified and minute expression of the eyes modified by a variety of words and phrases.[3]

Moreover, in many cases, the expression of the eyes is accompanied by the characters' eye behavior in *Sylvia's Lovers*, indicating their complicated relationship with one another. The characters' actions of looking at someone, how they look, and whom their eyes are directed to, are described in detail. As the title of the novel indicates, this is a story about

---

[1] See Bonaparte (1992), Suzue (2003), and Foster (2002). Suzue (2003: 448) wonders, in her afterword to *Sylvia's Lovers*, why Gaskell gives detailed scenery descriptions. Foster (2002: 155) praises *Sylvia's Lovers* for 'its melding of topographical vividness, historical interest and psychological perception.'

[2] For instance, in 'The Crooked Branch,' her 30-page short story published in 1859, Gaskell allots approximately one page to the explanation of the detailed geography of main characters' accommodation.

[3] Korte (1997: 204) points out that other body language in Gaskell's works is used to 'seek across to the thoughts, feelings, or attitudes of other characters through an observation of their body language' quoting from *North and South*.

Sylvia and her lovers: Kinraid, her former fiancé, and Philip, her husband. This complex love triangle with Sylvia, Kinraid, and Philip is closely related to their eye behavior. Sylvia falls in love with Kinraid, a specksioneer,[4] while Philip suffers from his unrequited love for her. It is interesting to note how Kinraid and Philip look at Sylvia, and how she reacts to the two men's gazes in different ways.

My focus in this paper is to explore characters' eyes and eye behavior in *Sylvia's Lovers*. My interest is to elucidate how the description of the characters' eyes and eye behavior is used to reveal their interpersonal relationships in the progress of the story.[5] Section 2 examines the collocational patterns used to describe the three main characters' eyes. Section 3 is directed to the eye behavior between Sylvia and Kinraid with reference to their relationship. In Section 4, I turn to an analysis of the eye behaviors in interactions between Sylvia and Philip to compare with that of Sylvia and Kinraid. Section 5 examines the scenes in which the three characters are together.[6]

2. Collocation of 'eyes'

This section is concerned with the collocational patterns of the characters' eyes. The collocations I treat here are limited to 'modifier + *eyes*.' The following table shows the collocations of 'eyes' for Sylvia, Philip and Kinraid. Though it is difficult to definitely classify modifiers based on their nature, I categorize them into two groups to reveal their features: outward appearances and inner states of mind. Moreover, modifiers concerned with inner states of mind are further divided into two categories: constant and temporary.

---

[4] 'Specksioneer' is an old word for 'whaler.'
[5] This novel can be divided into two parts, the earlier and the later part demarcated by the incident of Kinraid's disappearance.
[6] All quotations of *Sylvia's Lovers* are taken from Oxford edition. Italics in quotations are all mine. The electric text of *Sylvia's Lovers* was used to search the words related to eye(s). The correctness of the search results has been checked with printed texts. The electric texts of Gaskell's novels can be found at http://www.gutenberg.org/.

65

Table 1: Collocations of 'modifier + *eyes*'

Sylvia	physical		drooping eyes / gray eyes / steady dilated eyes / tearful eyes
	inner	constant	great soft eyes / miserable eyes / **pure eyes** / sweet trustful eyes /
		temporary	abstracted eyes / awful eyes / cold distrustful eyes / sad eyes / great wistful eyes / **sad eyes**
		constant + temporary	beautiful defiant eyes
Philip	physical		dark eyes / contracted eyes / **unseeing eyes**
	inner	constant	gentle wistful eyes
		temporary	passionate eyes / **sad hopeless eyes**
		constant + temporary	**discontented longing eyes** / wistful, eager eyes / wistful loving eyes
Kinraid	physical		hollow eyes / **quick eyes**/ beautiful sparkling eyes / bonny eyes
	inner	constant	none
		temporary	none
		constant + temporary	none

Analysis of the table above leads us the following observations.

First, as seen from the viewpoint of frequency, the collocational patterns of Sylvia's eyes appear 15 times in the story. Her 'modifier + *eyes*' are the most often described of any character: Philip's 'modifier + *eyes*' occurs 9 times and Kinraid's does 4 times.

Second, when we categorize modifiers into two groups (physical and inner), Sylvia is similar to Philip in the rate of the number of 'modifier + *eyes*.' Sylvia's 'modifier (physical) + *eyes*' occur 4 times and 'modifier (inner) + *eyes*' appears 11 times. Philip's examples (physical) also appear 3 times, and 6 examples are related to his inner state of mind. Modifiers connected with inner states of mind are more often used in their examples.

Third, in contrast to Sylvia and Philip, the collocations for Kinraid's eyes are unique compared to the others in that they only describe outward appearances. There is no example of his 'modifier (inner) + *eyes*' in the story. Consequently, it is difficult to observe Kinraid's mental states through his 'modifier + *eyes*.'

Fourth, among the three protagonists Sylvia's eyes are distinctive in the use of adjectives reflecting her emotions. For example, words with positive meanings such as 'soft,' 'pure,' and 'trustful' appear in the early part of the story. In contrast, modifiers such as 'discontented,' 'wistful,' 'sad,' and 'hopeless' are used to express Philip's negative feelings, while there are also some modifiers with positive meanings like 'gentle' and 'loving.' In addition, positive words like 'beautiful sparkling' and 'bonny' are utilized in description of Kinraid's eyes. Comparing Philip with Kinraid, though both positive and negative words related to inner states of mind appear in the former's description, there are no modifiers associated with inner states of mind in the latter's.

Fifth, I will discuss words containing some degree of ambiguity. It is difficult to determine whether Philip's 'unseeing eyes' should be categorized into outward appearance or inner state of mind.

(1) Philip came up to her [Hester], and stood looking at her with *unseeing eyes*; but the strange consciousness of his fixed stare made her uncomfortable, and called the faint flush to her pale cheeks, and at length compelled her, as it were, to speak, and break the spell of the silence. (Ch. 25)

Though Philip looks at Hester physically, he does not pay attention to her. A contradictory combination of words like 'looking' and 'unseeing' is used here.

Sixth, particular adjectives are used to describe multiple characters. 'Wistful' is applied to the descriptions of Sylvia, Philip, and Hester, who is Philip's co-worker. Especially, Philip tends to be depicted more repeatedly with 'wistful' than other characters: his eyes are 'gentle, wistful eyes' (Ch. 42), 'wistful eager eyes' (Ch. 44), and 'wistful loving eyes' (Ch. 45). 'Wistful' is used in combination with other adjectives. When he suffers a severe injury to his face in the war, his appearance is delineated as follows:

(2) He had saved some money from his allowance as bedesman and from his pension, and might occasionally have taken an outside place on a coach, had it not been that he shrank from the first look of every stranger upon his disfigured face. Yet *the gentle, wistful eyes*, and the white and faultless teeth always did away with the first impression as soon as people became a little acquainted with his appearance. (Ch. 42)

Though his face changes almost beyond recognition, the narrator says that his personality emerges from his eyes and teeth. In the other words, the collocation including a transferred epithet is used to indicate that Philip is a 'gentle' and 'wistful' person. I will discuss his other example of 'wistful' more in a later section.

'Wistful' is also used to describe Sylvia's eyes. Though Sylvia does not forgive Philip for his insincere deed, she expresses her gratitude for his kindness to her mother over the past years in her conversation with Kester, a farm-servant:

(3) Then she said,
     'Yet he were so good to mother; and mother loved him so. Oh, Kester!' lifting herself up, opening *her great wistful eyes*, 'it's well for folks as can die; they're spared a deal o' misery.' (Ch. 39)

'Great' means 'greatly' in this phrase to emphasize 'wistful' here. Her eyes are described as 'wistful,' suggesting her complicated feelings of thankfulness and regret, rather than just showing her rejection of him.

The way of using 'wistful' in Hester's description is similar to Philip's in that 'wistful' is used in combination with other adjectives (e.g. admiring):

(4) Then she held it on her hand, and turned it round about, putting her head on one side, the better to view the effect; and all this time, Hester, peeping at her through the folds of the stuffs displayed in Foster's windows, saw her with *admiring, wistful eyes*; wondering, too, if Philip, at the other counter, were aware of his cousin's being there, so near to him. (Ch. 11)

As mentioned above, we can observe the distinctive collocational patterns of each character's eyes.

3. Eye behavior between Sylvia and Kinraid

From Section 3 to 5, I will examine how main characters see or gaze at others in *Sylvia's Lovers*. Korte (1997: 58) points out that eye behavior provides 'information about the interactants and the nature of characters' interpersonal relations.' In addition, she divides their eye behavior into three types: (i) 'gaze (one person looking at another person),' (ii) 'mutual gaze or eye contact (two persons looking into one another's eyes),' and (iii) 'avoiding gaze' (Korte 1997: 58). I will observe characters' eye behavior in accordance with these three types.

This section is concerned with eye behavior between Sylvia and Kinraid. Their eye behavior fits the three patterns outlined by Korte. In the early part of the story, Kinraid's eye behavior pattern corresponds to (i) 'gaze,' while Sylvia's corresponds to (iii) 'avoiding gaze.' However, the pattern of their eye behavior changes from (i) and (iii) to (ii) as the plot develops. The following subsections examine their eye behavior in detail with examples.

3.1. Kinraid's eye behavior

This part focuses on Kinraid's eye behavior more closely. The pattern of his eye behavior is (i) 'gaze (one person looking at another person)' in the early part of the story. Kinraid keeps a constant eye on Sylvia during his visit to her house:

(5) *Kinraid's eye watched her* as she went backwards and forwards, to and fro, into the pantry, the back-kitchen, out of light into shade, out of the shadow into the broad firelight where *he could see and note her appearance.* (Ch. 9)

Passage (5) delineates how 'Kinraid's eye,' as the subject of the sentence, 'watched' Sylvia attentively wherever she goes without taking his eyes off her even for a moment. His eyes are used as a synecdoche here.

(6) 'Eh dear a' me!' said Bell, 'how well I mind yo'r telling me that tale! It were twenty-four year ago come October. I thought I never could think enough on a man as had rode on a whale's back!'

'Yo' may learn t' way of winnin' t' women,' said Daniel, winking at the specksioneer.

And *Kinraid immediately looked at Sylvia*. It was no premeditated action; it came as naturally as wakening in the morning when his sleep was ended; but Sylvia coloured as red as any rose at *his sudden glance*,—coloured so deeply that he *looked away* until he thought she had recovered her composure, and then *he sat gazing at her again*. (Ch. 9)

The characteristic feature of the passages above is the detailed depiction of Kinraid's passionate gaze towards Sylvia. In passage (6), Kinraid's eye movement is minutely detailed: 'Kinraid *immediately* looked at Sylvia,' 'his *sudden* glance' and 'he sat gazing at her *again*.' The words of visual perception modified by the adjective, 'sudden,' and the adverbs, 'immediately' and 'again' suggest that his act of watching her is intense and persistent.

Moreover, the use of simile that compares his eye movement with 'as waking in the morning' vividly illustrates that the action of his looking at her is habitual, rather than 'premeditated' behavior. The minute depiction of Kinraid's eye movement fluently reveals his attraction to Sylvia.

According to Korte's analysis, 'frequent and open glances are characteristic of dominating and extroverted personalities, but such glances are also seen to indicate honesty' (Korte 1997: 62). Kinraid observes Sylvia's reaction by gazing at her repeatedly. His eye behavior is dominant, and he seizes the initiative with their relationship. As mentioned in Section 2, though it is difficult to observe Kinraid's mental states because there is no example of his 'modifier (inner) + *eyes*' in the story, his eye behavior may suggest his inside thoughts.

3.2. Sylvia's eye behavior

Next, let us focus on Sylvia's eye behavior with reference to Kinraid. Characteristic of her eye behavior is (iii) 'avoiding gaze.' The following scene, describing Sylvia's visit to Kinraid with her father, reveals the way in which Sylvia as a young woman becomes conscious of Kinraid's eyes:

(7) Sylvia came towards, ruddy as any rose, and in a moment Kinraid recognized her as the pretty little girl he had seen crying so bitterly over Darley's grave.

70

He rose up out of true sailor's gallantry, as she shyly approached and stood by her father's side, *scarcely daring to lift her great soft eyes*, to have one fair gaze at his face. He had to support himself by one hand rested on the dresser, but she saw he was looking far better—younger, less haggard—than he had seemed to her before. His face was short and expressive; his complexion had been weatherbeaten and bronzed, though now he looked so pale; his eyes and hair were dark,—the former quick, deep-set, and penetrating; the latter curly, and almost in ringlets. His teeth gleamed white as he smiled at her, a pleasant friendly smile of recognition; but she only blushed the deeper, and *hung her head*. (Ch. 8)

In quotation (7), it is worth noting the process of her eye movement, our paying attention to the movement of her eyes and head: 'scarcely daring to lift her great soft eyes,' and 'hung her head.' Sylvia's eye behavior is depicted without using words related to 'seeing' directly. At first, Sylvia hesitates to meet Kinraid's gaze by 'scarcely daring to lift her great soft eyes.' According to Korte (1997: 62), 'avoiding gaze (or eye contact)' indicates 'fear, insecurity, or embarrassment.' Not lifting her eyes in this scene fits the pattern of 'avoiding gaze' that represents embarrassment. Differing from a direct negative, the expression 'scarcely daring to' implies her conflicting emotions. However, when she feels that she is being looked at by his 'quick, deep-set, and penetrating' eyes, she blushes 'the deeper,' and casts her eyes downward in embarrassment instead of making eye contact with him.[7]

Furthermore, Sylvia pretends not to notice Kinraid's gaze. The following quotations are further examples of her avoiding his gaze:

---

[7] In addition to her eye behavior, Sylvia's shyness is also marked by other body language in this scene: her 'standing by her father's side' reveals interpersonal distance and proximity: distance from Kinraid and dependence on her father. Sylvia's distinctive 'ruddy as any rose' complexion in quotation (7) is an outward representation of her shy disposition as marked by Kinraid. Her ruddy skin color changes into 'the deeper' blush under his gaze. Sylvia's movement of eyes, together with her change of complexion, signals her ambivalent feelings: her interest in seeing him and her embarrassment about keeping direct eye contact with him.

71

(8) 'But there's no need to tell me yo've getten a short memory.'
     'Why? what have I done? how dun you know it?'
     'Last night,' she began, and then she stopped, and *turned away her head, pretending to be busy in her daily duties of rinsing and such like.* (Ch. 15)

(9) 'I didn't think to see yo'. I thought yo'd ha' sailed.'
     'I told yo' I should come back, didn't I?' said he [Kinraid], still standing, with his hat in his hand, waiting to be asked to sit down; and she [Sylvia], in her bashfulness, forgetting to give the invitation, but, instead, *pretending to be attentively mending the stocking she held.* Neither could keep quiet and silent long. *She felt his eyes were upon her, watching every motion,* and grew more and more confused in her expression and behaviour. He was a little taken aback by the nature of his reception, and was not sure at first whether to take the great change in her manner, from what it had been when last he saw her, as a favourable symptom or otherwise. (Ch. 16)

Sylvia and Kinraid become acquainted at the New Year's party. After the party, they have a chance to meet each other. As seen in quotation (7), as well as quotations (8) and (9), Sylvia's eye behavior is not described with words related to 'seeing.' Instead, her avoidance of Kinraid's gaze is depicted with another expression. The phrases, 'turned away her head, pretending to be busy in her daily duties' and 'pretending to be attentively mending the stocking she held' indicate her avoiding his gaze with feelings of embarrassment.

Sylvia's early eye behavior is characterized by a casting down of her eyes to avoid direct eye contact out of shyness and embarrassment, rather than a total avoidance of his gaze. However, in the following passage, their eye behavior is different from that previously examined:

(10) *She looked up at him defiantly*, and set her red lips firm. He enjoyed her determination not to reply to this question; it showed she felt its significance. *Her pure eyes looked steadily into his*; nor was the expression in his such as to daunt her or make her afraid. They were like two children defying each other; each determined to conquer. (Ch. 15)

Instead of casting her eyes downward, Sylvia 'looked up at him' and fixed

72

'her pure eyes steadily in to his [eyes.]' They try to 'read' one another's inner states through such fixed gazing 'like two children defying each other.' Their protracted and direct eye contact indicates an increased closeness in their relationship. This scene occurs just before their engagement, and their intense mutual gaze might be considered as 'an important signal for romantic love.'[8]

3.3. The change in eye behavior between Sylvia and Kinraid

As we saw in earlier subsections, the pattern of eye behavior in interactions between Sylvia and Kinraid can be summarized in accordance with Korte's definition as follows: the combination of Kinraid's 'gaze' and Sylvia's 'avoiding his gaze' repeatedly appears in the early part of the story. While Kinraid keeps a steady gaze on Sylvia for a prolonged period, she does not meet his gaze. The detailed description of their eye behavior visually represents Kinraid's attraction to Sylvia and her embarrassment under his gaze.[9]

However, the early repeated pattern of their eye behavior (the combination of (i) 'gaze' and (iii) 'avoiding gaze') changes into the pattern (ii) 'mutual gaze or eye contact (two persons looking into one another's eyes)' in the latter part of the story. This subsection examines this aspect of their eye behavior.

Kinraid and Sylvia's cordial relationship suddenly comes to an end in the later part of the novel when Kinraid is abducted by a press-gang. The following scene describes the eye behavior of Sylvia and Kinraid when he unexpectedly appears before her eyes after three years absence. Observe how the depiction of their eyes and their movements (in italics) in (11) and (12) differ from the examples we have seen above:

(11)　'Sylvia!' he said, in a voice tremulous with joy and passionate love. 'Sylvia!'
　　　She looked round; he had turned a little, so that the light fell straight on his

---

[8] See Korte (1997: 58).
[9] The pattern of a woman blushing and casting down her eyes under a man's gaze is representative of conventional body language seen in the sentimental novels in the eighteenth century as examined by Ikeda (2018).

73

face. It was bronzed, and the lines were strengthened; but it was the same face she had last seen in Haytersbank Gully three long years ago, and had never thought to see in life again.

He was close to her and held out his fond arms; she went fluttering towards their embrace, as if drawn by the old fascination; but when she felt them close round her, she started away, and cried out with a great pitiful shriek, and put her hands up to her forehead as if trying to clear away some bewildering mist.

Then she looked at him once more, a terrible story in her eyes, if he could but have read it.

Twice she opened her stiff lips to speak, and twice the words were overwhelmed by the surges of her misery, which bore them back into the depths of her heart. (Ch. 33)

In this scene, Sylvia's inner confusion is vividly demonstrated by her eye behavior, which illustrates the process of her recognizing his face, and then remembering her miserable fate. First, she 'looked round' to see his face clearly in the light. The second look reveals 'a terrible story' for him to 'read.' This means that the message of her irretrievable fatal error is to be imparted to him not by the actual words but by means of her manners of looking at him.

As Sylvia thought that Kinraid was dead at sea, she was absolutely petrified at his sudden reappearance. Sylvia is too stunned to utter words, and just looks at him as if he were a ghostly apparition.[10] The dreadful moment of reunion continues:

(12)   Sylvia took her hands away from her face; it was gray as the face of death; *her awful eyes were passionless* in her despair.

'Where have yo' been?' she asked, in slow, hoarse tones, as if her voice were half strangled within her.

'Been!' said he, *a red light coming into his eyes, as he bent his looks upon her*; now, indeed, a true and not an assumed suspicion entering his mind. [. . .] Between every clause of this speech he paused and gasped for her answer; but none came. *Her eyes dilated and held his steady gaze prisoner*

---

[10] The tittle of Chapter 33 is 'An apparition.' This word means a ghost or an unexpected appearance by someone.

74

as with a magical charm—neither could look away from the other's wild, searching gaze. When he had ended, she was silent for a moment, then she cried out, shrill and fierce,—
'Philip!' No answer.
Wilder and shriller still, 'Philip!' she cried. (Ch. 33)

A state of absolute confusion is suggested by the description of eyes and eye behavior. Her 'dilated' eyes, widened by intense emotions, are fixed on his 'steady gaze' making it prisoner with a magical charm.[11] Unable to get a verbal answer from Sylvia, Kinraid, with a 'wild, searching gaze,' tries to 'read' Sylvia's inner state through her eyes. The repetition of 'gaze,' a fixed and intent look, represents an intense moment of communication by means of eye contact. The red light coming into his eyes symbolizes his suspicion about their past promise of marriage. It can be noted that this longer stare is completely different from a romantic mutual gaze illustrated earlier. Compare this passage with the quotation in (10), in which Sylvia looks at Kinraid with her 'pure' eyes, and attempts to guess his feelings as if they are 'like two children defying each other.' Contrastively, in this scene, her eyes are delineated with the adjectives 'awful' and 'passionless.'[12]

In the early part of the story, their eye behavior develops a regular pattern: Kinraid gazes at Sylvia openly, and she avoids his gaze from embarrassment. However, in the latter part of the story, the set pattern of their eye behavior breaks down: they gaze into each other's eyes to examine each other's intentions. Kinraid's gaze changes little in nature throughout the story. In contrast, the quality of Sylvia's eye behavior changes along with her growth. When she is young, she avoids Kinraid's gaze in embarrassment; however, she uses eye contact to convey her feelings. Their relationship may be partly described through the eye behavior mentioned above.

---

[11] Sylvia's 'dilated' eyes are also seen in other scenes: 'Her eyes dilated, her lips blanched, her pale cheeks grew yet paler' (Ch. 26); 'her steady, dilated eyes had kept him [Philip] dumb and motionless as if by a spell' (Ch. 31).
[12] In this scene, Sylvia's complexion is depicted as 'gray as the face of death.' This description contrasts with her earlier 'ruddy as a rose' countenance.

4. Eye behavior between Sylvia and Philip

In this section, I turn to the analysis of the eye behavior used in describing interactions between Sylvia and Philip, in an attempt to draw distinctions between that of Sylvia and Kinraid. The pattern of Sylvia's eye behavior toward Philip corresponds to (iii) 'avoiding gaze,' and Philip's eye behavior toward her may be categorized as (i) 'gaze.' Feeling deeply attracted to her, both Philip and Kinraid gaze at her, while Sylvia tends to avoid their gaze, but for different reasons and in different ways.

4.1. Philip's eye behavior toward Sylvia

This part examines Philip's eye behavior toward Sylvia. As mentioned in Section 3.1., though Kinraid also gazes at Sylvia repeatedly, he watches her openly to let her recognize his gaze. The pattern of his eye behavior applies to (i) 'gaze.' However, Philip's eye behavior is different from Kinraid's in terms of quality. There are a variety of descriptions of Philip's repeated and consistent eye behavior toward Sylvia:

(13) But she knew that it was not her own poor self that attracted *his lingering gaze*. (Ch. 25)

(14) . . . the strange consciousness of *his fixed stare made her uncomfortable*, ... (Ch. 25)

(15) . . . she knew from past experience that cousin Philip *always stared at* her. (Ch. 4)

(16) . . . and Sylvia was aware that his [Philip's] eyes followed her about with knowing looks *all the evening*. (Ch. 12)

(17) . . . *he watched her with discontented, longing eyes*, and grew more inclined *every moment*, ... (Ch. 12)

(18) . . . not too be too far off to *be gazed at by eyes that caressed her every moment*. (Ch. 20)

(19) . . . Philip seemed only pretences for taking *stolen glances* at Sylvia. (Ch. 10)

(20) His *stealthy glance* did not meet her eye; . . . . (Ch. 43)

Different types of nouns and verbs of perception ('gaze,' 'stare,' and 'glance')[13] are used to demonstrate Philip's obsession with Sylvia. 'Gaze'

---

[13] *OED2* defines 'gaze' as 'the act of looking fixedly or intently; a steady or intent look' (*OED2* s.v. Gaze n. 2.), and 'stare' as 'to gaze fixedly and with eyes

76

and 'stare' indicate his fixed look. The use of modifiers like 'lingering' and 'fixed' together with words and phrases such as 'always,' 'all the evening,' and 'every moment' are linked to words of perception, intensifying his continuous attachment. In quotations (19) and (20), his 'glance,' a brief or hurried look, is illustrated together with words like 'stolen' and 'stealthy.' Different from Kinraid's case, Philip keeps monitoring Sylvia obsessively whether or not she notices him. Philip's eye behavior toward Sylvia stands in contrast to Kinraid's. Such a fixed and intent action even makes her 'uncomfortable.'

4.2. Sylvia's eye behavior toward Philip
Next, I examine Sylvia's eye behavior toward Philip. The pattern of eye behavior between Philip and Sylvia is a combination of (i) 'gaze' and (iii) 'avoiding gaze' like that between Kinraid and Sylvia in the early part of the story.

As discussed in earlier sections, when she is conscious of Kinraid's gaze, she blushes and casts her eyes downward. Yet in the case of Philip, Sylvia avoids his gaze out of irritation and unfavorable feeling. At the beginning of the story, she responds negatively and has no friendly feelings towards Philip, often irritated by his words. One of the most outstanding descriptions of his one-sided gazing at Sylvia is found in the following scene:

(21) *All this Philip could see*; the greater part for her [Sylvia's] face was lost to him as *she half averted it*, with a shy dislike to the way in which she knew from *past experience* that cousin Philip *always stared* at her. And *avert* it as she *would* she heard with *silent petulance* the harsh screech of Philip's chair as he heavily dragged it on the stone floor, sitting on it all the while, and felt that he was moving round so as to *look at* her as much as *was in his power*, without absolutely turning his back on either her father or mother. (Ch. 4)

Philip continues to 'look at' Sylvia in spite of her rejection of his stare. It is suggested that there is a repeated pattern of their eye behavior: his

---

wide open' (*OED2* s.v. Stare v. 1.a.), while 'glance' is signified as 'a brief or hurried look' (*OED2* s.v. Glance n. 4.).

'stare' and her 'averting.' Verbs of perception such as 'see,' 'stare' and 'look at' are linked to other words and phrases like 'always,' and 'as much as was in his power.' These expressions represent his prolonged and repeated gaze. On the other hand, as for Sylvia, her eye movement from 'half averted it [her face]' to 'avert it' and the use of 'would' indicate her constant avoidance of his stare. This movement to evade his gaze is a sign of her mental distance from him. The harsh screech of Philip's chair indicates his obsessive desire to catch her glance even if she averts her face. The sound he makes, together with his eye behaviors, allows the reader to imagine the tense situation more clearly.

4.3. The change in eye behavior between Sylvia and Philip

This section is concerned with the change in eye behavior between Sylvia and Philip. As mentioned in earlier subsections, the pattern of eye behavior between Sylvia and Philip is similar to that between Sylvia and Kinraid in that Philip gazes at her, with her consciously attempting to avoid his gaze. However, her avoidance of Kinraid's gaze has a positive implication, while her avoidance of Philip's implies a negative one.[14]

In the latter part of the story, their eye behavior changes in accordance with the development of the plot. The pattern of Sylvia's eye behavior toward Philip changes from (iii) 'avoiding gaze' to (ii) 'mutual gaze or eye contact.'

When Kinraid was abducted by the press-gang, he asked Philip to give a message of love to Sylvia. However, Philip, instead of delivering it, married her. The following scene describes her eye behavior after discovering his dishonest betrayal:

(22) She rose to her feet, but staggered when she tried to walk; her *glazed eyes* fell upon Philip as he instinctively made a step to hold her steady. *No light came into her eyes* any more than if she had *looked upon a perfect stranger*; not even was there the contraction of dislike. Some other figure filled her mind, and she *saw* him no more than she *saw the inanimate table*. That way

---

[14] Korte (1997: 62) points out that the avoidance of eye contact means fear, insecurity, or embarrassment. Sylvia's avoidance of eye contact with Philip implies 'insecurity.'

of looking at him withered him up *more than any sign of aversion would have done.* (Ch. 34)

What attracts our attention in this scene is the description of Sylvia's eyes and eye behavior. Her eyes are depicted as 'glazed eyes' with 'no light.' Moreover, the comparative expression 'no more than' is used, representing the way in which she looks upon him: as if he were 'a perfect stranger' and an 'inanimate table.' This suggests that she does not feel any emotions like 'dislike' or 'aversion,' but rather a feeling of helpless desperation.[15] Though Sylvia avoids Philip's gaze because of her aversion to him when she is young, she makes eye contact with him as she grows older.[16]

From the beginning of the story, Philip gazes at Sylvia constantly and stealthily. She sometimes notices his gaze and is irritated by it. In the latter part of the story, the eye behavior changes from 'gaze' to 'peep.'

After the stunning disclosure of his lies, Philip also disappears from Sylvia's sight. Near the end of the novel, the narrator tells the reader that he is severely wounded in the war, and hides himself to peep at his wife and daughter from the shadow of the corner of a house. The following passage describes how Philip, like a vagabond, takes a stealthy look at his wife and daughter, whose attention is focused on a street circus:

(24) When he came to the angle of junction between the lane and the High Street, he seemed plunged all at once into the very centre of the bustle, and he drew himself up into a corner of *deep shadow*, from whence he could *look out* upon the street. [. . .] A circus was making its grand entry into Monkshaven, with all the pomp of colour and of noise that it could muster. [. . .] *All this Philip might have seen*; did see, in fact; but heeded not one jot. Almost

---

[15] This paper limits itself to the analysis of eye behavior among protagonists. However, after separated from the two men, there are some scenes where Sylvia gazes at the sky, fire, and the sea: 'Then she gazed out at the evening sky. . . .' (Ch. 32); '. . . and Sylvia sat *gazing at the fire* with abstracted eyes, thinking of the past year. . .' (Ch. 24); '. . . *gazing abroad* over the wide still expanse of *the open sea*' (Ch. 30).

[16] Sylvia and Philip gaze at each other to forgive each other's faults. In the last chapter, Sylvia gazes at Philip's 'wistful loving eyes' before his death (Ch. 45).

opposite to him, not ten yards apart, standing on the raised step at the well-known shop door, was Sylvia, holding a child, a merry dancing child, up in her arms to see the show. She too, Sylvia, was laughing for pleasure, and for sympathy with pleasure. She held the little Bella aloft that the child might *see* the gaudy procession the better and the longer, *looking at* it herself with red lips apart and white teeth *glancing* through; then she turned to speak to some one behind her—Coulson, as Philip *saw* the moment afterwards; his answer made her laugh once again. *Philip saw it all. . . .* (Ch. 42)

The manner of Philip's looking is conspicuous. He looks over the whole scene, including Sylvia, who watches the procession of the circus with a smile, cradling the baby in her arms. She is unaware of Philip's hidden gaze, as he covertly watches her from 'a corner of deep shadow.' Among the crowd of people gathered to see the circus procession, Philip's eyes are focused on just one point: on Sylvia and his daughter. Furthermore, their eyes are directed to different directions and his unilateral gaze is never to be met by hers. Interestingly, a series of similar phrases are repeated to suggest his eye behavior as an ardent spectator observing the entire scene: 'All this Philip might have seen' and 'Philip saw it all.' The similar instance is also seen in (21): 'All this Philip could see.'

Philip's act of lonely peeping is exemplified in the following passage:

(25) . . . he could see with *his wistful, eager eyes* the shape of the windows—the window of the very room in which his wife and child slept, unheeding of him, the hungry, broken-hearted outcast. (Ch. 44)

He sees the town with 'wistful, eager eyes' when he returns to his hometown after the war. The act of his peeping is also linked to the description of his wistful eyes. As already mentioned in Section 2, 'The gentle, wistful eyes' are distinctive even in his disfigured face after his serious injury in the war. The adjective 'wistful,' indicating mournful eagerness, is suggestive of his painful emotion.[17] In quotation (24), he

---

[17] *OED2* defines 'wistful' as 'expectantly or yearningly eager, watchful, or intent; mournfully expectant or longing. (Chiefly in reference to the look.)' (*OED2* s.v. Wistful 2.). As for other examples: 'Yet the gentle *wistful eyes*, and the white and faultless teeth always did away with the first impression as soon as people became

80

looks eagerly at the house where his wife and daughter live. 'Eager' expresses his temporary emotion of longing to see his family. Therefore, 'wistful, eager eyes' describe his personality and temporary feeling together.

Philip keeps on secretly watching his wife and daughter until his death, without their eyes ever meeting. Example (26) illustrates the last scene of the novel in which Philip dies in Sylvia's arms:

(26) Then Hester bore her child to her, and Sylvia opened wide *her miserable eyes*, and only *stared, as if all sense was gone from her*. (Ch. 45)

Sylvia's eyes are depicted as 'miserable eyes' along with the use of simile, 'as if all sense was gone from her.' The adjective 'miserable' is used as the transferred epithet describing her life of 'misery.'[18] Compared with the description of her innocent, bright eyes in the earlier part of the novel, we find a distinctive change in quality of adjectives modifying Sylvia's eyes in the later part: 'miserable' (Ch. 45) and 'glazed' (Ch. 34) with reference to Philip, as well as 'dilated' (Ch. 33), 'awful' (Ch. 33), and 'passionless' (Ch. 33) for Kinraid. Sylvia's eyes filled with emotion turn to hopeless glassy eyes as the plot develops.

5. Eye behavior between Sylvia and her lovers

In the last section, let us examine the scenes where Sylvia and her lovers are together. In the novel, there are some scenes in which Sylvia, Philip, and Kinraid are together at one place. In particular, their eye behavior towards one another is described impressively in scenes related to the New Years' party. In these scenes, we can see the three patterns which Korte points out concurrently. Sylvia conceals herself behind a screen, feeling the men watching her:

(27)   But, for all her screen, *she felt a pair of eyes were fixed upon her with a glow of admiration deepening their honest brightness*. Somehow, look in what direction she would, she caught the glance of those eyes before she

---

a little acquainted with his appearance' (Ch. 42).

[18] In the preceding chapter, Sylvia refers to her life as 'misery' (Ch. 39).

could see anything else. So *she played with her apron-strings, and tried not to feel so conscious.* There were another pair of eyes,—not such *beautiful, sparkling eyes,—deep-set, earnest, sad, nay, even gloomy, watching* her every movement; but of this she was not aware. (Ch. 12)

In quotation (27), the pattern (i) 'gaze' and (iii) 'avoiding gaze' appear in the description of eye behavior. Kinraid's and Philip's eye behavior toward her is depicted contrastively. Two pairs of eyes fixed on Sylvia are delineated in a way to characterize her lovers. First, Sylvia is conscious that Kinraid gazes at her intently and favorably ('with a glow of admiration deepening their [eyes'] honest brightness'). Wherever she looks, 'she caught the glance of those eyes before she could see anything else,' which suggests Kinraid's constant gazing at her. As we have seen in quotations (8) and (9), in which she 'pretends' to be occupied with household chores to conceal her feelings, her playing 'with her apron-strings' is also a reaction to hide her embarrassment under his enthusiastic eyes. The detailed description of her external appearance serves to reveal her inner state. This also suggests the author's preference for details.

The narrator also refers to the existence of another pair of eyes, which Sylvia is not aware. In contrast to Kinraid's 'beautiful' and 'sparkling' eyes with 'honest brightness,' Philip's eyes are depicted as 'deep-set, earnest, sad, nay, even gloomy.' It is worth noting that Philip's eye behavior is characterized as those of a 'spectator,' '*watching* her every movement.'

Meanwhile, 'both Kinraid and Philip find it difficult to keep their eyes off her' (Ch. 12). Kinraid has 'a secret triumph' (Ch. 12), while Philip gets more and more suspicious as he sees 'her soft eyes averted from him after the first glance' (Ch. 12). In quotation (28), patterns (i) and (ii) apply to their eye behavior:

(28) There was something in Sylvia's look, ay, and in Charley Kinraid's, too, that shot conviction into Philip's mind. *He watched them incessantly* during the interval before supper; they [Sylvia and Kinraid] were intimate, and yet shy with each other, in a manner that enraged while it bewildered Philip. What was Charley saying to her in that whispered voice, as they passed each other?

82

Why did they linger near each other? Why did Sylvia *look so dreamily happy*, so startled at every call of the game, as if recalled from some pleasant idea? Why did *Kinraid's eyes always seek her* while *hers were averted, or downcast*, and her cheeks all aflame? Philip's dark brow grew darker as he *gazed*. (Ch. 12)

As marked by 'ay' in the first line, the whole passage is revealed through Philip's perspective. The eye movement among three persons vividly illustrates their personal relationship. There are double layers of eye behavior: the eye movement between Sylvia and Kinraid, and Philip's gaze monitoring their movement. Through his careful reading, Philip notices that the eye behavior between Kinraid and Sylvia—Kinraid's constant gaze and Sylvia's casting her eyes blushingly as demonstrated in Section 2—suggests their close relationship. The shift in verbs of visual perception from 'watch' to 'gaze,' indicating Philip's more fixed eye behavior, corresponds to his change in feelings from suspicion to a conviction of Kinraid and Sylvia's intimacy. The description of his physical appearance—'dark brow grew darker as he gazed'—is also a sign of his deeper anxiety. By a series of questions without reported clauses ('Why did *Kinraid's eyes always seek her* while *hers were averted, or downcast*, and her cheeks all aflame?'), we are allowed access to his state of mind. Philip's confused mind comes to the fore by means of free indirect thought.[19] Considering the fact that the intimate eye movement between Sylvia and Kinraid triggers Philip's jealous suspicion, leading to successively tragic circumstances, eye behavior plays an active part in the progress of the story.

6. Final Remarks
As I have discussed, Gaskell's fastidiousness with detail is reflected in the description of the characters' eyes and eye behavior in *Sylvia's Lovers*. The following can be summarized from the foregoing survey.

First, my attention has focused on the collocational patterns of characters' eyes. In doing so, it becomes clear that a variety of adjectives are used to describe their eyes, thus reflecting their temperament.

---

[19] See Leech and Short (1981: 342–8).

Second, I examined characters' eye behavior in accordance with Korte's patterns of eye behavior. The principal characters, Sylvia, Philip, and Kinraid, have some regular patterns of eye behavior. The different manners of eye behavior between Sylvia and her lovers represent their intricate interrelationships. Kinraid gazes at Sylvia openly, while Philip does so stealthy.

Moreover, the depiction of eyes and eye behavior changes in the latter part of the story. In the earlier part, it is used to express interpersonal feelings. However, after Kinraid's disappearance and the disclosure of Philip's betrayal, it is more closely integrated in the darker plot of their miserable fate.

Lastly, the characteristic features of representation are found in the way the author uses a variety of words and phrases, including simile and comparative expression, to depict eye behavior. The characters' eyes and eye behavior often function as a means of communication in lieu of actual words, revealing their feelings as well as their interpersonal relationships.

My future research will be to conduct further analyses of the characters' eyes and eye behavior in Gaskell's other works, and to elucidate her use of body language systematically. I hope that such investigation and analysis may lead to the establishment of a whole system and understanding of the functions of body language in the history of English expression in literature.

References

Bonaparte, Felicia. 1992. *The Gypsy-Bachelor of Manchester: The life of Mrs. Gaskell's demon*. Charlottesville: University Press of Virginia.

Chapple, J. A. V. & Arthur Pollard. (ed.). 1997. *The letters of Mrs. Gaskell*. Manchester: Mandolin.

Foster, Shirley. 2002. *Elizabeth Gaskell: A literary life*. New York: Palgrave Macmillan.

Gaskell, Elizabeth. 1999. *Sylvia's Lovers*. Andrew Sanders. (ed.). Oxford: Oxford University Press. Akiko Suzue (trans.). 2003. *Shirubia no koibitotachi* (in Japanese). Osaka: Osaka Kyoiku Tosho.

Hirono, Yumiko. 2008. *Shisen wa hito wo korosuka* [*Can the eye be a killer?*]. Kyoto: Minerva Shobo.

Hori, Masahiro. 2004. *Investigating Dickens' style: A collocational analysis.* New York: Palgrave Macmillan.

Ikeda, Yuko. 2018. From convention to creation: Blushing in Jane Austen with reference to her predecessors. *A Chronological and Comparative Study of Body Language in English and American Literature.* Tokyo: Kaitakusha. 41–62.

Korte, Barbara. 1997. *Body language in literature.* Tronto: University of Tronto Press.

Leech, Geoffrey N. & Michael H. Short. 1981. *Style in fiction: A linguistic introduction to English fictional prose.* London: Longman.

Saiki, Aiko. 2010. Eyes in *Sylvia's Lovers. Elizabeth Gaskell and the tradition of English literature.* Osaka: Osaka Kyoiku Tosho. 45–54.

Uglow, Jenny. 1993. *Elizabeth Gaskell: A habit of stories.* London: Faber and Faber.

Body Language in Dickens's *Hard Times*: The Characters' Eyes and Eye Behavior

Masahiro Hori

1. Introduction

Charles Dickens (1812–70) often gives the description of a character's eyes as one of the devices for characterization, which he particularly uses to delineate evil or abnormal persons. Uriah Heep in *David Copperfield* (1849–50) who 'had hardly any eyebrows, and no eyelashes, and eyes of a red-brow,' is suggestively portrayed as a hypocritical young man with eyes like a fox, while Bill Sikes's 'two scowling eyes' in *Oliver Twist* (1837) and Mrs. Jelleby's 'choking eyes' in *Bleak House* (1852–3) are suitable in describing a rogue and an unusual person. In addition, Dickens also describes the behavior of seeing or looking at someone or something. In such cases, the act of viewing can often be as significant as the depiction of the physical appearance of a character's eyes, which is one Dickensian device indispensable for characterization. Considering these descriptions from the point of the development of modern English prose, they may be regarded as one of Dickens's innovative or creative techniques, as they scarcely appear in the works of the originators of the English novel, such as Defoe, Smollett, Fielding, etc.[1]

In *Hard Times* (1854), especially, which has more insistent or definite intention than any other of Dickens's novels,[2] we cannot help but notice

---

[1] Hori (2004: 18–23).

[2] It is very familiar that F. R. Leavis classes *Hard Times* as a moral fable and states that 'I need say no more by way of defining the moral fable than that in it

86

the significance of the characters' eyes. Therefore, the purpose of this paper is to show how the characters' eyes are described, and how their acts of viewing are connected with characterization and the theme in *Hard Times*. First, I will survey the descriptions of the main characters' eyes which not only contribute to characterization, but also convey symbolic meanings having close relations with the world of Fact or Fancy as one of the subjects in this novel.[3] Secondly, the delineations of the characters' acts of viewing will be examined. What kind of verb occurs with high frequency? How, whom or what do they look at? Here I will survey the verbs 'see' and 'look,' and the words and phrases related to them. Finally, I will discuss the difference of significance in the text between the uses of the perception verbs 'see' and 'look,' which respectively connect significantly with the theme.[4]

2. The collocation 'adjective + *eyes*'

Before launching into an exhaustive study of the characters' eyes and eye behavior in *Hard Times*, a brief survey of characteristics of collocations in Dickens may be useful for considering his collocations in the movement of the language of English fiction. His collocations show not only a greater variety of collocations, but also far more unique patterns of collocations than those of representative authors of 18th century English fiction. As an example, in the collocation 'adjective + *eyes*,' Defoe's *Robison Crusoe*, Smollett's *Roderick Random*, Fielding's *Tom Jones*, and Richardson's *Pamela*[5] will be compared with *Hard Times*.

The functions of the collocation 'adjective + *eyes*' in characterization could be classified into the following five functional categories:

---

the intention is peculiarly insistent . . . .' (F.R. Leavis 1962: 259)

[3] 'The opposition of Fact and Fancy in *Hard Times* also results in a structured contrast between different kinds of and attitudes towards fiction.' Connor (1985: 95)

[4] All the quotations from *Hard Times* are from *The Oxford Illustrated Dickens*.

[5] All the quotations from Defoe's *Robinson Crusoe*, Smollett's *Roderick Random*, Fielding's *Tom Jones*, and Richardson's *Pamela* are taken from the *ECF*.

(A) the physical appearance of *eyes*: *little eyes*
(B) the impression of *eyes*: *charming eyes*
(C) a portrait of the temporary feeling expressed through *eyes*: *angry eyes*
(D) a portrait of a permanent personality expressed through *eyes*: *honest eyes*
(E) the others: *farsighted eyes*

Function (A) refers to the physical or outward appearance such as the size and color of a person's eyes. In Function (B), the beauty and attraction of a person's eyes are impressively or subjectively depicted. Function (C) describes a person's temporary feeling or emotion expressed through his or her eyes. Function (D) represents a person's comparatively permanent personality expressed through his or her eyes. As for Functions (C) and (D), these types of collocation can be rhetorically called a transferred epithet. That is to say, the adjective 'angry' or 'honest' grammatically qualifies the noun *eyes* but literally or semantically applies to the holder or possessor of *eyes*. Any other types of 'adjective + *eyes*' will be dealt with as Function (E).

In Defoe's *Robinson Crusoe* we can hardly find any descriptions of a character's eyes. There are only the following two instances:

(A) *two broad shining eyes*
(B) None.
(C) None.
(D) None.
(E) *the same eyes*

From the five functions mentioned above these could be said to be instances of Function (A) and Function (E). The rarity of collocations of adjectives with the word *eyes* may indicate that 'Defoe's emphasis is all . . . on the difficulty of exact, objective description, on the problem of getting the shade just right, not on the author's momentary feelings toward the subject' (Adolph 1968: 280–1).

Smollett's *Roderick Random* also does not have many instances of collocations of the word *eyes*. We find the following instances:

(A) *little grey eyes, lively blue eyes, dim eyes*
(B) *languid eyes, aged eyes, fierce eyes, enchanting eyes, owlish eyes, ravished eyes*

88

(C) None.
(D) None.
(E) *many eyes*

In terms of number, *Roderick Random* has more examples of this collocation than *Robinson Crusoe*; however, there are no examples expressing a temporary feeling (Function C) or a comparatively permanent personality trait of a character (Function D) represented through his or her eyes.

In Fielding's *Tom Jones* we find more examples than *Robinson Crusoe* or *Roderick Random,* but it bears similarity to these works in that functions C and D are not found:

(A) *black eyes, bright eyes, dim eyes, dry eyes, large eyes, moistened eyes, shining eyes, sloe-black eyes, sparkling eyes, staring eyes, swollen eyes, uplifted eyes*
(B) *fiery eyes, languid eyes, prettiest eyes, profane eyes, pure eyes, strongest eyes, unhallowed eyes*
(C) None.
(D) None.
(E) None.

Richardson's collocations are far richer than those of other 18th century English fiction authors in terms of this type of collocation. He gives a variety of depictions of feelings and personalities through his characters' eyes in *Pamela*:

(A) *black eyes, red eyes, saucer eyes, staring eyes, tearful eyes*
(B) *charming eyes, dear eyes, favourable eyes, fiery eyes, fine eyes, pretty eyes, speaking eyes, sweet eyes*
(C) *delighted ones* (eyes), *half-affrighted eyes, pleased eyes*
(D) *foolish eyes, watchful eyes, worthy eyes*
(E) *different eyes, an hundred eyes, these surrounding eyes, weak eyes*

In *Pamela* we come across many collocations of *eyes* that express characters' feelings, states of mind and personalities. Some of these collocations, such as *speaking eyes, sweet eyes* and *worthy eyes,* are unusual or deviant collocations. Such unusual collocations are more frequently used in Richardson's later novel *Clarissa.* Therefore, even just in his use of unusual collocations of 'adjective + *eyes*' we could say that Korte's following comments are much to the point:

> Richardson's work is generally regarded as a turning point in the history of the novel, and this is also evident in his use of NVC (non-verbal communication). It is with Richardson that a novel tradition begins to emerge in which the expressive potential of body language can be exploited to the full. (Korte 1997: 184)

We have so far made a brief survey of the representative works of the four originators of the English novel for the collocation of 'adjective + *eyes.*' Next, I would like to examine this type of collocation in Dickens' *Hard Times* (1854). It is the shortest of Dickens' novels and its approximate word-tokens are 104,000 words, while those of the 18th century English four novels examined here, *Robinson Crusoe, Roderick Random, Tom Jones,* and *Pamela* are approximately 124,000 words, 191,000 words, 350,000 words, and 220,000 words respectively. Therefore, *Hard Times* is the least of these five novels in the number of word-tokens, but shows the most abundant variety of the collocation 'adjective + *eyes.*'

(A) *cavernous eyes, deep-set eyes, black eyes, dark eyes, blinking eyes, moistened eyes, winking eyes*
(B) *classical eyes, thinking eyes, searching eyes, eager eyes*
(C) *distracted eyes, woeful eyes, bold eyes*
(D) *cold eyes, trusting eyes, confiding eyes, gentle eyes, pleasant eyes, not too sober eyes, practiced eyes*
(E) *both eyes, all eyes, many eyes*

The following characteristics with the collocation of 'adjective + *eyes*' in Dickens' *Hard Times* may be deduced from the above table. For one thing, Dickens might be said to continue and develop Richardson's techniques of collocations in terms of collocations of *eyes,* as all of the five collocational functions are found in *Hard Times,* just as they are in

Richardson's *Pamela*. For another, some unusual collocations, such as *classical eyes* and *practiced eyes,* and such a metaphorical collocation as *cavernous eyes* for characterization are not found in the other four novels. The following collocations are used only in *Hard Times* according to *ECF* (Eighteenth Century Fiction on CD-ROM)[6] and *NCF* (Nineteenth Century Fiction on CD-ROM)[7].

cavernous eyes, classical eyes, trusting eyes, confiding eyes, woeful eyes, sober eyes, thinking eyes, winking eyes, searching eyes, eager eyes, practiced eyes

We have so far examined the collocations of 'adjective + *eyes*' in the four novels of the four originators of the English novel and Dickens' *Hard Times*. Dickens' collocations show not only a greater variety of collocations but also far more unique patterns of collocations than those of other authors of 18th century English fiction. Because this research is limited in the number of works and the types of collocation, we need to expand the subjects of this research. We could say, however, that this richness of collocation in Dickens may be considered his contribution to the development of the language of English fiction and hence that there would be some possibility of research from the chronological viewpoint of expressions in literature.

3. The characters' eyes
In this section I will discuss the physical appearance of eyes, which Dickens often describes to individualize a person.

3.1. Mr. Gradgrind's eyes
Mr. Gradgrind's way of thought or personality is metaphorically expressed by his forehead, eyebrows, and eyes as in the following:

---

[6] This database comprises the works of 30 of the most influential writers of the British Isles in the eighteenth century. It contains 77 collected works or 96 discrete items.
[7] This database contains 250 complete works of prose fiction by 109 authors from the period 1781 to 1901.

91

(1) The emphasis was helped by *the speaker's square wall of a forehead*, which had his eyebrows for its base, while *his eyes found commodious cellarage in two dark caves, overshadowed by the wall*. (I, 1)

Here his forehead means 'Head' as opposed to 'Heart,' as seen in Dickens's working notes (Stone ed. 1987: 247–61), and the wall which overshadows his eyes is a head obsessed with the doctrine of facts. His eyes cannot see the world of heart, that is, a person's kind or sincere feelings due to his obsession with the doctrine of facts. Therefore, the symbolic description of Mr. Gradgrind's eyes in the first chapter of Book I of this work may already suggest that 'the basic movement of the novel originates in the spiritual blindness of Gradgrind, ...' (Sucksmith 1970: 157).

Consider the following figurative instances:

(2) 'Whether,' said Mr. Gradgrind, pondering with his hands in his pockets, and *his cavernous eyes* on the fire, ... (I, 4)

(3) At about this point, *Mr. Gradgrind's eyes* would fall upon her; and *under the influence of that wintry piece of fact*, she would become torpid again (I, 9).

The phrase, 'that wintry piece of fact' is a figurative expression for Mr. Gradgrind's eyes, which are wintry, lacking warmth or comfort, and with which he obsesses over facts.

3.2. Josiah Bounderby's eyes

Josiah Bounderby's eyes, a part of his balloon-like appearance, are described with hyperbolic phrases, which are an indicator of his inflated self-esteem.

(4) A man with a great puffed head and forehead, swelled veins in his temples, and such a strained skin to his face that *it seemed to hold his eyes open, and lift his eyebrows up*. A man with a pervading appearance on him of being inflated *like a balloon*, and ready to start. (I, 4).

While in the case of Mr. Gradgrind the narrator uses obvious but quite

92

complicated metaphors, the simile 'like a balloon' in the passage above is employed; however, the narrator's pervading technique of expression is hyperbole, and his description of Bounderby's eyes as being wider or longer open than they are, works to create an image of eyes that are alert and watchful, but at the same time sly.[8]

3.3. Mrs. Sparsit's eyes

The color of Mrs. Sparsit's eyes is expressed by the adjectives 'black' and 'dark' as in the sentences that follow:

(5) . . . she kept *her black eyes* wide open, with no touch of pity, with no touch of compunction, all absorbed in interest. (II, 10)

(6) With *her dark eyes* and her hook nose warily in advance of her, Mrs. Sparsit softly crushed her way through the thick undergrowth, ... (II, 11)

(7) . . . plain to *the dark eyes of her mind*, as the electric wires which ruled a colossal strip of music-paper out of the evening sky, were plain to *the dark eyes of her body*, ... (II, 11)

The transferred epithets in which an adjective grammatically modifying one noun literally or semantically applies to another in the sentence shows her emotion and pride as used in the following:

(8) Mr. Bounderby, under the influence of this difficult adjuration, backed up by *her compassionate eye*, could only scratch his head in a feeble and ridiculous manner, ... (II, 11)

(9) . . . so severely wide awake were *those classical eyes of hers*, and so impossible did it seem that her rigid nose could yield to any relaxing influence, ... (II, 9)

(10) In the first instant of alighting, Mrs. Sparsit turned *her distracted eyes* towards the waiting coaches, ... (II, 11)

---

[8] *OED2* defines 'open-eyed' as 'having the mental 'eyes' or perceptive powers open' (*OED2* s.v. Open-eyed 2.).

And her eyes are metaphorically expressed as given below:

(11) Mrs. Sparsit, ... kept such a sharp look-out, . . . that *her eyes, like a couple of lighthouses on an iron-bound coast,* . . . . (II, 9)

(12) 'If not quite!' said Mrs. Sparsit, straining *her hawk's eyes* to the utmost. (II, 10)

(13) The smaller birds might have tumbled out of their nests, fascinated by *the glittering of Mrs. Sparsit's eyes* in the gloom, as she stopped and listened.[9] (II, 11)

3.4. Bitzer's eyes

Bitzer's eyes are characterized by the adjectives 'light' and 'cold' as follows:

(14) . . . the boy was so *light-eyed* and light-haired that the self-same rays appeared to draw out of him what little colour he ever possessed. (I, 2)

(15) *His cold eyes* would hardly have been eyes, but for the short ends of lashes which, by bringing them into immediate contrast with something paler than themselves, expressed their form. (I, 2)

Moreover, the movement of Bitzer's eyes are described in the following sentence:

(16) Bitzer, after *rapidly blinking at Thomas Gradgrind with both eyes* at once, and so catching the light upon his quivering ends of lashes that they looked like the antennae of busy insects, ... (I, 2)

Needless to say, the usage of the sun or a sunbeam symbolizes the world of Heart or Fancy, and the eyes suggest the gate to the world of Heart.

---

[9] It is subsequently hinted that Louisa is one of the smaller birds fascinated by the hawk's eyes of Mrs. Sparsit.

94

3.5. Sissy's eyes

In contrast with Bitzer's eyes, Sissy's eyes, which are modified by the transferred epithets, are considered an indicator of a heart full of sincere feelings as in the following:

(17) . . . the sweet face [Sissy's face] with *the trusting eyes*, made paler than watching and sympathy made it, by the rich dark hair. (II, 9)

(18) He [Harthouse] added in his mind, 'And you speak to him with *the most confiding eyes* I ever saw, and the most earnest voice (though so quiet) I ever heard.' (II, 2)

Whereas Bitzer's eyes are incapable of capturing light, Sissy's eyes amply absorb sunlight, as described in the following:

(19) . . . whereas the girl was *so dark-eyed* and dark-haired, that she seemed to receive a deeper and more lustrous colour from the sun, when it shone upon her, ... (I, 2)

3.6. Mr. Sleary's eyes

A kind-hearted circus proprietor, Mr. Sleary's eyes are described with a literal contrast as in the following:

(20) Last of all appeared Mr. Sleary: a stout man as already mentioned, with *one fixed eye*, and *one loose eye*, ... (I, 6)

(21) With that he regarded her attentively with *his fixed eye*, surveyed his company with *his loose one*, ... (I, 6)

The literal contrast between 'fixed' and 'loose' may reflect the character of Mr. Sleary, who reveals truth in his loose way of thought with a fixed confidence. [10] Some words which are contextually synonymous with

---

[10] Mr. Sleary makes Mr. Gradgrind understand according to his peculiar thinking that the world of Fancy is essential to human life: 'People mutht be amuthed. They can't be alwayth a learning, nor yet they can't be alwayth a working, they an't made for it.' (III, 8)

95

'loose' are seen in the following:

(22) Mr. Sleary, . . . conveyed no more expression into *his locomotive eye* than into his fixed one. (III, 7)

(23) Mr. Sleary, who with his mouth open and *his rolling eye* as immovably jammed in his head as his fixed one, ... (III, 8)

(24) As they were all going out again, he favoured her with one slight roll of *his movable eye*, desiring her to linger behind. (III, 8)

(25) . . . and Mr. Sleary instructing him, with *his one practicable eye*, that Bitzer was the object of his particular attentions. (III, 8)

4. The characters' acts of viewing
What is of interest in this section is how Dickens describes the behavior of seeing or looking when a character sees or looks at someone or something rather than the depiction of the physical appearance of a character's eyes. That is to say, this section will pay attention to the delineation of the characters' eye behavior.

4.1. Louisa's eye behavior
The representations of raising or lowering the characters' eyes are significant in the text. They do not only imply characters' states of mind, but sometimes have symbolic meanings, as may be detected in the following instance:

(26) He [Bounderby] spoke of young Thomas, but he looked at Louisa.
    'We were peeping at the circus,' muttered Louisa, haughtily, *without lifting up her eyes*, 'and father caught us.' (I, 4)

The author tells us Louisa's state of mind (internal perspective) by using the word 'haughtily' followed by an external perspective (Fowler 1977: 89–103), with the description of her lowered eyes. As in general the avoidance of eye contact makes a powerful statement about interpersonal relationships (Korte 1997: 61), her lowered eyes suggest her unfriendly

96

attitude toward Bounderby, as she is 'rubbing the cheek he [Bounderby] had kissed, with her handkerchief, until it was burning red' (I, 3).

Contrastively Louisa's raised eyes contain a symbolic significance as illustrated in the following:

(27) She [Louisa] fell upon her knees, and clinging to this stroller's child *looked up at her* [Sissy] *almost with veneration.* (III, 1)

Her act of looking up at Sissy is depicted with the adverbial phrase 'with veneration' referring to her internal state of mind. Her raised eyes may suggest that Sissy is just like a goddess or a savior for Louisa, who is absolutely heartbroken after partially escaping the evil influences of Harthouse.

This raised eye behavior might relate to or imply a divine reality such as the Lord and God, as discussed in Watanabe (2018), one of this collection's academic papers. The following is from the last scene of this work relating to her father's change of heart:

(28) He [Mr. Gradgrind] *raised his eyes to where she* [Sissy] *stood, like a good fairy in his house*, and said in a tone of softened gratitude and grateful kindness, 'It is always you, my child I' (III, 7)

In this citation, Sissy is also represented as divine reality.[11]

4.2. Louisa and Tom's eye behavior

In *Hard Times*, Louisa and Tom are contrastively characterized in the description of their behavior of looking. As the story progresses, the contrast becomes more striking. Though he delineates the appearance of Mr. Gradgrind's and Bounderby's eyes as suggestive of their thoughts in the beginning of the text, in introducing Louisa and Tom, the narrator describes their acts of looking as in the following:

---

[11] Stephen Blackpool, who seems to play a martyr in our text like Saint Stephen the protomartyr, dies 'looking upward at the star' and 'gazing at a star' (III, 6). His act of looking is symbolic, too. Here the star may suggest the eye or the light of God.

(29) (Mr. Gradgrind finds Louisa and Tom peeping into the circus and calls to them.)

'Louisa!! Thomas!!' Both rose, red and disconcerted. But, *Louisa looked at her father with more boldness than Thomas did.* Indeed, *Thomas did not look at him,* but gave himself up to be taken home like a machine. (I, 3)

Louisa and Tom both feel confused or embarrassed when they are caught peeping into the circus by their father, and their acts of looking are described with the same verb and sentence structure. Their eye behavior is, however, different. That is, there is a complete contrast in description as Louisa's act of looking is described affirmatively, while Tom's is described negatively. That is to say, Louisa's direct looking at her father and Tom's lack or avoidance of eye contact with his father imply powerful but different statements about their respective interpersonal relationships with their father. These different acts of looking do not only show their differing attitudes toward their father, but also suggest the different fates they will meet, though they may both be considered victims of their father's upbringing.

In addition, as he grows older, Tom develops an increasing tendency to lower his eyes as seen in the following:

(30) *He had long been a down-looking young fellow,* but this characteristic had so increased of late, that he never raised his eyes to any face for three seconds together. (II, 11)

But this characteristic eye behavior increases further when he commits a crime, after which he is incapable of glancing up at his father:

(31) . . . and from time to time, *he turned the whites of his eyes restlessly and impatiently towards his father.* (III, 7)

This implies a fear of his father, a lack of self-confidence and his dishonesty, rather than his habit of looking. Then, the narrator represents his eyes with the adverbs 'restlessly' and 'impatiently' referring to his states of mind. Similarly, the adverbs in the following sentence convey changes in his psychological state:

98

(32) (James Harthouse's smooth words and tricky attitude easily put Tom off his guard.)
He [Tom] *looked at his companion* [Harthouse] *sneakingly, he looked at him admiringly, he looked at him boldly*, and put up one leg on the sofa (II, 3).

On the other hand, Louisa does not 'see' but rather 'looks' straight at her father, using her eyes consciously and with attention:

(33) From the beginning, she had sat *looking at him fixedly*. (I, 15)

(34) . . . she, with a hand upon his shoulder, *looking fixedly in his face*. (II, 12)

(35) . . . she . . . *still looking fixedly in his face*, went on. (II, 12)

In the sentences above, Louisa's manner of looking at her father is described with the verb 'look' and emphasized with the adverb 'fixedly.' Why or with what purpose does she look at him? We can easily assume that Louisa's eyes are searching for something in Mr. Gradgrind. In the work, Louisa's searching eyes are turned not only to Mr. Gradgrind, but also to Sissy and Harthouse, as given below:

(36) She sat, *looking down*; but, at this question, *raised her eyes searchingly and a little resentfully*, [toward Harthouse] (II, 7)

(37) 'At least, what?' said Louisa, *with her searching eyes upon her* [Sissy]. (III, 1)

(38) 'And he liked them?' said Louisa, *with a searching gaze on Sissy all this time.* (I, 9)

Moreover, Louisa very often keeps her eyes fixed on the fire, too, as in the following:

(39) His sister [Louisa] sat in the darker corner by the fireside, now looking at him, *now looking at the bright sparks as they dropped upon the hearth.* (I, 8)

(40) Louisa . . . *looked again at the short-lived sparks* that so soon subsided into ashes. (I, 14)

Her act of looking at the fire has in a way the same significance as when she looks at her father: she looks at the fire 'as if she were reading what she asked, in the fire, and it were not quite plainly written' (I, 8). But her eyes cannot elicit answers to her silent questions from her father, Harthouse, or Sissy, much less from the fire.

4.3. Mrs. Sparsit's eye behavior

The narrator does not describe the physical appearance or impression of Louisa's eyes, but rather the behavior of looking mainly through the use of the verb 'look.' Contrastingly, he not only variously describes the physical appearance of the hawk's dark eyes of Mrs. Sparsit's, as mentioned in 3.3., but also includes the various aspects of her eye behavior as if to indicate that she is spying on Louisa and Harthouse. Consider the verbs employed for Mrs. Sparsit's acts of seeing or looking:

(41) i) See + Object—*seeing them* [Louisa and Harthouse] (III, 5) / *saw the changes of the face* he [Harthouse] had studied (II, 10) / In the interest of *seeing her* [Louisa] (II, 10)

ii) See + Object + to Verb—*saw James Harthouse come and go* / *saw him detain* her with encircling arm (II, 11) / *had seen her sit* (II, 11) / *saw her out of the wood*, and *saw her enter the house* (II, 11)

iii) See + Object + Verb-ing—*saw him languishing* down the street on the shady side of the way (II, 1) / *saw Louisa still descending* (II, 10) / *saw Louisa coming* (II, 10)

iv) Watch + Object (or Verb-ing)—*watched him* last (II, 11) / *watching his looks* (II, 11) / to *watch Louisa coming down* (II, 10)

v) Keep + Object (Noun of Viewing)—*kept her wary gaze* upon the stairs (II, 10) / *kept unwinking watch and ward* (II, 11) / *kept such a sharp look-out* (II, 9)

When Mrs. Sparsit spies on Louisa and Harthouse, the narrator does not use the verb 'look at' but most frequently the verb 'see' and the verb 'watch' and the form 'keep + Object (Noun of Viewing).'

4.4. Sissy's eye behavior

A clown's daughter in Sleary's circus, Sissy, who holds the opposite position regarding Mr. Gradgrind's utilitarian theories, sometimes uses her eyes to produce a 'wondering look' when presented with Mr. Gradgrind's theories in 'Never Wonder' (I, 8). Her eyes often are much more powerful and meaningful than her words. Consider the following:

(42) Her mother had taken it rather as a disturbance than otherwise, to be visited, as she reclined upon her sofa; young people, Louisa felt herself all unfit for; Sissy she [Louisa] had never softened to again, since the night when *the stroller's child* [Sissy] *had raised her eyes to look at Mr. Bounderby's intended wife* [Louisa]. (II, 9)

Here Louisa understands Sissy's eye movement to mean that Mr. Bounderby is not a person whom Louisa would heartily like to marry. And Louisa herself knows her heart. That is, Sissy's eyes may be Louisa's heart. Furthermore, her eyes do not submit to Harthouse's cynical smile as in below:

(43) *James Harthouse looked at her with an incredulous smile upon his lips; but her mind looked over and beyond him,* and the smile was quite thrown away. (III, 2)

Sissy looks over and beyond him, ignoring his affected or unnatural smile. Then, the metonymy 'her mind,' used for 'Sissy' in 'her mind looked over and beyond him,' may suggest her resolute behavior of looking.

4.5. Mr. Gradgrind's eye behavior
Mr. Gradgrind's act of looking is expressed with nominal construction, in which the adjectives are expressive of his personality, as follows:

(44) His eminently practical friend [Mr. Gradgrind], on seeing him, stopped also, and gave Louisa *a reproachful look that plainly said, 'Behold your Bounderby!'* (I, 4)

His reproachful look intends to force Louisa to behold Bounderby, but implies her studious avoidance as well. Additionally, his eye behavior toward her suggests his consideration of Bounderby, her intended husband. The description of Mr. Gradgrind's eye behavior also serves to illuminate his inner state, as seen in the following:

(45)　'Stop a bit!' cried Bounderby, who all this time had been standing, as before, on the hearth, bursting at the very furniture of the room with explosive humility.

　　　'You have one of those strollers' children in the school.'

　　　'Cecilia Jupe, by name,' said Mr. Gradgrind, with something of *a stricken look at his friend.*

　　　'Now, stop a bit!' cried Bounderby again. 'How did she come there?'

　　　'Why, the fact is, I saw the girl myself, for the first time, only just now. She specially applied here at the house to be admitted, as not regularly belonging to our town, and - yes, you are right, Bounderby, you are right.' (I, 4)

Mr. Gradgrind's stricken look at Bounderby not only expresses his astonishment, but also implies a kind of defensiveness that he has nothing to do with the presence of Sissy in this house.

Moreover, his act of seeing is expressed with unusual collocation and periphrasis as shown in the following:

(46) The speaker [Mr. Gradgrind] . . . *swept with their eyes the inclined plane of little vessels* . . . . (I, 1)

(47) Mr. Gradgrind, . . . *had no need to cast an eye upon the teeming myriads of human beings around him,* . . . .　(I, 15)

The phrase, 'the inclined plane of little vessels' means the pupils at Gradgrind's school. To him, the pupils are equal to little vessels lain in a line from the viewpoint of Fact. The phrases 'had no need to cast an eye upon' and 'swept with his eyes' can be replaced with 'ignored' or 'did not care about.' That is to say, he is blind to their human nature, personality, and imagination in the world of Fancy.

5. The significances of the verbs *see* and *look*

I will shift my focus of attention to the perception verbs 'see' and 'look' which have different or contrastive significances.

102

5.1. The verb *see*

In the world of Fact represented by Mr. Gradgrind, to see is only 'to perceive light, colour, external objects and their movements with the eyes' (*OED2* s.v. See 1.a.). Let us take as typical the instance of the verb 'see' in the world of Fact:

(48)   'I'll explain to you, then,' said the gentleman, after another and a dismal pause, 'why you wouldn't paper a room with representations of horses. *Do you ever see horses walking up and down the sides of rooms in reality—in fact?* Do you?'
'Yes, sir!' from one half. 'No, sir!' from the other.
'Of course no,' said the gentleman, with an indignant look at the wrong half.
'Why, then, you are *not to see anywhere, what you don't see in fact*; What is called Taste, is only another name for Fact.' Thomas Gradgrind nodded his approbation. (I, 2)

The verb 'see' in the above citation is never 'to perceive mentally an immaterial object, a quality, etc. or apprehend by thought a truth' (*OED2* s.v. See 3.a. (fig)). In that sense, Louisa's act of looking which intends to draw some answer from her father and the fire, as we have observed in section 4.2. of this paper, may be in defiance of Mr. Gradgrind's principles. The following is a natural consequence in the world of Fact:

(49) *No little Gradgrind had ever seen a face in the moon*; it was up in the moon before it could speak distinctly. (I, 3)

To see a face in the moon is to perceive an immaterial object through the faculty of imagination, based on the experience of the world of Fancy found in nursery rhymes and fairy tales. Mr. Gradgrind, who lives in the word of Fact, does not allow fairy stories or nursery rhymes into his children's nursery. At the last sight of his disgraced son, however, Tom is dressed in the costume of a circus performer playing in a dramatized version of Jack the Giant Killer, symbolizing that he is psychologically aided by the world of Fancy, but not of Fact. This is a bitter irony (cf. Sucksmith 1970: 248).

5.2. Mr. Gradgrind's 'seeing' and Louisa's 'looking'

The eye actions of Mr. Gradgrind are expressed with the verb 'see.' 'See' is distinguished from the verb 'look,' which is applied in the case of Louisa, who always turns or fixes her searching attention or regard (*OED2* s.v. Look 3. Fig. a.), as has been shown in the previous section. Let us consider how Mr. Gradgrind 'sees' when Louisa 'looks at' him in the sentence which follows:

(50) (Louisa escaping with her wounded heart comes back to seek refuge with Mr. Gradgrind.)
He might have added more than all, *when he saw the face* [Louisa's face] *now looking at him.* (III, 1)

Mr. Gradgrind's act of seeing Louisa looking at him implies a recognition of what is before his eyes (that is, not Louisa but her face), but also indicates his inability to understand what the act of her looking at him suggests. That is to say, the verb 'see' means only to perceive an external object. In other words, the premise that to see is to know or to understand does not hold true in the case of Mr. Gradgrind. There is some contrast between Louisa's and Mr. Gradgrind's acts of viewing in the following:

(51) (When Louisa hears of Mr. Bounderby's proposal of marriage, Mr. Gradgrind is momentarily surprised at her expressionless face.)
From the beginning, *she had sat looking at him fixedly.* As he now leaned back in his chair, and *bent his deep-set eyes upon her in his turn*, perhaps *he might have seen one wavering moment in her*, when she was impelled to throw herself upon his breast, and give him the pent-up confidences of her heart. (I, 15)

Louisa's act of looking at him fixedly reflects her mental attitude toward her father, while in the case of Mr. Gradgrind only the physical movement of his eyes is described without the use of the verb 'see' or 'look.' This implies that he fails to notice what her eyes are searching for. In other words, his act of seeing is not to mentally perceive something, but to experience something with the eyes.

There is, too, some interchange in the use of 'look' and 'see' between

104

Louisa and Mr. Gradgrind:

(52) ' . . . What would Mr. Bounderby say?'
At the mention of this name, *his daughter stole a look at him*, remarkable for its intense and searching character. *He saw nothing of it, for before he looked at her she had again cast down her eyes!* (I, 3)

5.3. Mr. Gradgrind's change of eye behavior
We observe a change in Mr. Gradgrind's act of viewing as given below:

(53) (Mr. Gradgrind notices the failure of his theories when Louisa falls into a faint.)
And he laid her down there, and *saw the pride of his heart and the triumph of his system, lying, and insensible heap, at his feet.* (II, 12)

In the world of Fact 'see' means to perceive only external objects. But in the above sentence, it collocates the immaterial objects 'the pride of his heart' and 'the triumph of his system' which stand for Louisa and, at the same time, are indicative of Mr. Gradgrind's states of mind, very rarely described through the text. Therefore, the change of the use of the verb 'see' may be regarded as a change in his character. This seems to be contrasted, however, with the verb 'look' employed for Louisa, which being agentive and dynamic, indicates an intentional activity (Quirk *et al* 1985: 204). In other words, his acts of seeing are a passive activity only to express a state of perception, and he does not look at Louisa herself but rather into his heart and the collapse of his system. However, when Mr. Gradgrind's and Louisa's eyes are turned to the same direction, their acts of looking have an important symbolic implication, as described below:

(54) Louisa returned with her father. Standing hand-in-hand, *they both looked down upon the solemn countenance* [Stephen]. (III, 6)

6. Final Remarks
The foregoing arguments have focused on how Dickens tries to make use of the descriptions of the characters' eyes not only as one of the devices for characterization, but also as cues for their ways of thinking and for

105

their roles in *Hard Times*, and how he uses a variety or repetition of expressions to represent the acts of viewing, which vary according to the characters. Lastly, the significance the perception verbs 'see' and 'look' have in relating closely to the theme of the text was noted. It is hoped that the above survey, though tentative and limited, may show how the representation of the eyes and eye behaviors is instrumental in bringing about some characteristic or innovative aspects of Dickens's language[12] in the development of modern English prose style. And it may also lead us in a new direction to an exhaustive study of the descriptions of the characters' eyes and eye behaviors as part of body language in literature, to make a significant contribution to a chronological study of body language in historical stylistics.

References

Adamson, Sylvia. 1999. The literary language. In S. Romaine (ed.), *The Cambridge history of the English language Volume 4: 1776–1997*, 589–692. Cambridge: Cambridge University Press.

_____. 2000. The literary language. In R. Lass (ed.), *The Cambridge history of the English language, Volume 3: 1476–1776*. Cambridge: Cambridge University Press, 539–653.

Adolph, Robert. 1968. *The Rise of Modern Prose Style*. Cambridge, MA: MIT Press.

Biber, Douglas & Edward Finegan. 1988. Drift in three English genres from the 18th to the 20th centuries: a multidimensional approach. In M. Kytö, O. Ihalainen & M. Rissanen (eds.), *Corpus linguistics, hard and soft*. Amsterdam: Rodopi, 83–101.

Blake, Norman. 1992. The literary language. N. Blake (ed.) *The Cambridge history of the English language Volume 2: 1066–1476*. Cambridge: Cambridge University Press, 500–41.

---

[12] For example, in *Dombey and Son* (1846–8) Mr. Dombey's eyes, which are always attracted to little Paul, show that his son becomes the center of his life. Additional examples include Florence's looking at Mr. Dombey as a symbol of the love she offers timidly to her father, and Paul's gaze at Florence with a continuous confidence as representing eternity. The verb 'see' and its variation in the language of *Dombey and Son* might be another possible subject of study.

106

Bray, Joe. 2014. A portrait of historical stylistics. In P. Stockwell & S. Whiteley (eds.), *The Cambridge handbook of sylistics*. Cambridge: Cambridge University Press.

Brook, G. L. 1970. *The language of Dickens*. London: André Deutsch.

Busse, Beatrix. 2014. (New) Historical stylistics. In M. Burke (ed.), *The Rutledge handbook of stylistics*. London: Rutledge.

_____. 2016. New historical stylistics. In V. Sotirova (ed.), *The Bloomsbury companion to stylistics*. London: Bloomsbury Academic.

Chambers, Raymond Wilson. 1963. *On the continuity of English prose from Alfred to More and his school*, London: Oxford University Press.

Connor, Steven. 1985. *Charles Dickens*. Oxford: Basil Blackwell.

Fowler, Roger. 1977. *Linguistics and the novel*. London: Methuen.

Godden, Malcolm. 1992. Literary language. In R. Hogg (ed.), *The Cambridge history of the English language Volume 1: The beginning to 1066.* Cambridge: Cambridge University Press, 490–535.

Hori, Masahiro. 1992. Some stylistic observations on the Characters' eyes and acts of viewing in Dickens's *Hard Times*. A collection of essays in commemoration of the 50th anniversary of Kumamoto Gakuen.

_____. 2004. *Investigating Dickens' style: A collocational analysis*. New York: Palgrave Macmillan.

Korte, Barbara. 1997. *Body language in literature*. Toronto: University of Toronto Press.

Leavis, F. R. 1962. *The great tradition*. Harmondsworth: Penguin Books.

Leech, Geoffrey & Mick Short. 2007. *Style in fiction: A linguistic introduction to English fictional prose* 2nd edition. London: Longman.

Mahlberg, Michaela. 2013. *Corpus stylistics and Dickens's fiction*. New York: Routledge.

McMaster, Juliet. 2004. *Reading the body in eighteenth-century novel*. Basingstoke: Palgrave Macmillan.

Monod, Sylvere. 1968. *Dickens the novelist*. Norman: University of Oklahoma Press.

Poplawski, Paul (ed.). 2001. *Writing the body in D. H. Lawrence: Essays on language, representation, and rexuality*. London: Greenwood Press.

Quirk, Randolph. 1974. *The linguist and the English language*. London: Edward Arnold.

Sørensen, Knud. 1985. *Charles Dickens: Linguistic innovator*. Aarhus: Arkona.

Sucksmith, Harvey. 1970. *The narrative art of Charles Dickens*. Oxford: The Clarendon Press.

Stone, Harry (ed.). 1987. *Dickens' working notes for his novels*. Chicago: The University of Chicago Press.

Yamamoto, Tadao. 1950 (2003). *Growth and system of the language of Dickens: An introduction to A Dickens lexicon* 3rd edition. Hiroshima: Keisuisha.

Databases

Eighteenth-Century Fiction on CD-ROM (ECF) 1996. Chadwyck-Healey.

Nineteenth-Century Fiction on CD-ROM (NCF) 2000. Chadwyck-Healey.

Body Language in Dickens with Special Reference to 'Hand'

Keisuke Koguchi

1. Introduction

Korte (1997: 7) states, in her elaborate work *Body Language in Literature*, that Charles Dickens (1812–70) is one of the authors who 'are notorious for their excessive use of body language,' and so 'the reader encounters body language on almost every page.' Among words indicative of bodily parts, such as 'hand,' 'face,' or 'eye,' according to Hori (2004: 118–20), the word 'hand' is employed with the highest frequency in Dickens's works.[1] Moreover, it has been observed that as a public speaker, Dickens gave 'additional force and meaning to what he said' by the use of 'his wonderfully expressive hands,' and there is additional evidence that he made unusually frequent use of gesture in private conversation.'[2]

A careful examination of the contrastive and repetitive use of the word 'hand' and its co-occurring words between characters or contexts reveals some of Dickens's stylistic devices that we are liable to overlook, such as devices to individualize characters, suggest their states of mind, or make a scene more concrete and vivid. My particular attention in this paper is directed toward three different usages of the word 'hand': first, the

---

[1] In the following section, I will also show my own statistical data on high-frequency words in Dickens's works. Additionally, in the present paper, when I refer to word frequency, I consider this in conjunction with lemmatization, which means that the words are assigned to their base form.

[2] Page (1988: 155), quoting Justin McCarthy.

110

construction of 'modifiers + hand,' second, the construction of 'verb + hand,' especially the combination of 'rub + hands,' and third, the repetitive use of the word 'hand' through which a scene is made vivid or visually concrete. This analysis will contribute to a fuller understanding and appreciation of Dickens's stylistic and linguistic techniques in describing his characters.

2. Dickens use of words referring to body parts

Here, before examining Dickens's creative use of the word 'hand,' I investigate the author's preference for bodily words through corpus-based research.

Table 1 below illustrates the 50 highest-frequency content words in the *Dickens Corpus* of his 23 works, and in the *19th Works Corpus*, which is composed of 74 works from eleven 19th-century authors excluding Dickens. The total number of words in the *Dickens Corpus* is approximately 4.5 million, while the *19th Works Corpus* has approximately 13.5 million words.[3] In my own corpora, I consider word lemmatization: that is to say, the word 'say' in Table 1 contains the word-forms 'say,' 'said,' and 'saying'; the word 'young' includes 'young,' 'younger,' and 'youngest'; when I mention the frequency of the word 'hand,' this includes the frequency of its plural form 'hands.' This is mandated by my interest in the repetition of words of the same form.[4]

As Table 1 shows, nouns related to body parts, 'hand,' 'head,' 'eye,' and 'face,' are employed at higher frequencies in the *Dickens Corpus* compared with the *19th Works Corpus*; particularly, the word 'hand' is at

---

[3] The works of each corpus are shown in Appendix. I have basically followed the procedure by which Hori (2004: 117–20) created a corpus of content words for 23 of Dickens's works. According to the procedure, 'the following types of words have been removed from the wordlist: function words (pronouns, articles, prepositions, conjunctions, auxiliaries, and relatives) and proper nouns. In addition to these removals, words having different parts of speech, such as have, had (auxiliary and verb), so (conjunction, adverb, pronoun) and do (verb and auxiliary) are also omitted as they are highly frequent in numerous texts and registers and thus, similar to function words, show no distinctive features among particular texts or registers.'

[4] For the purpose of this study I used AntConc 3.2.4w (http://www.antlab. sci.waseda.ac.jp/software.html) as concordance software.

Rank 17 in the former corpus, while it is at Rank 35 in the latter corpus. The table does not present ranks of the other three body words, 'eye,' 'face,' or 'head' in the *19th Works Corpus*, but each word is, respectively, at Rank 60 with 12,736 instances, at Rank 81 with 10,282 instances, and at Rank 101 with 9,011 instances.

Table 1 may not provide sufficient or adequate statistical data on the word frequencies of Dickens's or 19th-century authors' works, but at least it does indicate Dickens's predilection for these bodily words in describing his characters.

Table 1. The 50 highest-frequency content words in the *Dickens Corpus* and the *19th Works Corpus*

Dickens Corpus		19th Works Corpus		Rank	Dickens Corpus		19th Works Corpus	
App. 4,499,000 words		App. 13,534,000 words			Dickens Corpus		App. 13,534,000 words	
Rank	**Word**	**Freq.**	**Word**	**Freq.**	**Rank**	**Word**	**Freq.**	**Word**	**Freq.**
1	say	39,657	say	92,503	26	again	6,919	other	21,639
2	no	16,235	no	51,410	27	other	6,884	give	20,890
3	go	14,521	go	42,352	28	much	6,736	day	20,539
4	know	13,810	know	39,508	29	great	6,704	much	20,042
5	look	13,492	think	39,307	30	such	6,665	tell	19,730
6	very	12,770	man	36,301	31	well	6,384	only	19,651
7	good	12,197	good	35,497	32	head	6,367	never	19,119
8	man	11,982	see	35,411	33	eye	6,263	old	18,088
9	see	11,685	come	32,938	34	dear	6,260	get	17,710
10	come	11,527	make	32,516	35	day	6,137	hand	17,391
11	little	11,296	very	32,146	36	get	6,099	house	16,491
12	take	10,790	more	29,440	37	way	5,794	way	15,610
13	time	9,926	now	28,971	38	gentleman	5,786	again	15,362
14	think	9,861	take	27,624	39	face	5,682	great	15,337
15	make	9,751	look	26,650	40	young	5,628	two	14,982
16	old	9,275	any	24,122	41	house	5,278	young	14,759
17	hand	9,196	time	24,036	42	give	5,240	word	14,549
18	more	9,110	like	23,784	43	two	5,225	thing	14,435
19	now	8,917	then	23,639	44	return	5,190	too	14,102
20	some	8,235	little	23,608	45	night	5,158	woman	13,801
21	then	7,622	some	23,331	46	lady	5,013	find	13,778
22	any	7,559	such	22,914	47	tell	5,002	friend	13,585
23	like	7,290	lady	22,195	48	door	4,965	here	13,524
24	here	7,254	own	21,869	49	own	4,953	hear	13,388
25	never	6,926	well	21,867	50	long	4,893	room	13,196

Furthermore, in order to demonstrate Dickens's preference for such body part nouns as 'hand,' 'head,' 'eye,' and 'face,' compare their frequencies between the *Dickens Corpus* and the *19th Works Corpus*, and

112

moreover, the *18th Works Corpus*, which consists of 31 works from ten 18th-century authors.

Table 2 below shows the frequencies of the four body part nouns in the three different corpora. The three corpora are of different sizes, so each frequency is converted into a value per million words, normalizing the frequency scores.

Table 2. Frequencies of 'hand,' 'head,' 'eye,' and 'face' in the three corpora

Word	Dickens Corpus Approx. 4,499,000 words		19th Works Corpus Approx. 13,534,000 words		18th Works Corpus Approx. 5,111,000 words	
	Freq.	/1M	Freq.	/1M	Freq.	/1M
hand	9,196	2,044	17,391	1,285	5,189	1,015
head	6,367	1,415	9,011	666	2,738	536
eye	6,263	1,392	12,736	941	2,996	586
face	5,682	1,263	10,282	760	1,600	313

Table 2 shows that such body part nouns as 'hand,' 'head,' 'eye,' and 'face' are more frequently used in the works of 19th-century authors than those of 18th-century authors. The statistical data of Table 2 support Korte's claims (1997: 182–3):

(1) The extent to which novelists' awareness of body language and its expressive quality has increased since the mid-eighteenth century is obvious. . . . Increased attention to body language in the nineteenth century also becomes obvious in that it is often strongly emphasized—through detailed description, a glossing or comments, or conspicuously poetic presentation.

Furthermore, it is said that the normalized figures per million words in Table 2 statistically demonstrate Dickens's strong preference for the four body part nouns, compared with 18th- and 19th-century authors in the descriptions of the characters. Among the four words, especially, the body part noun 'hand' is most frequently used in the three corpora.

3. Collocations of 'hand' in *OT* and *TTC*

In this section, my attention is focused on collocational patterns of the word 'hand' in describing characters in two of Dickens's novels, that is to say, *Oliver Twist* (1837–9), which is regarded as one of his early works, and *A Tale of Two Cities* (1859), one of his later works. I focus upon what words modify the word 'hand' in the descriptions of characters of the two works. The analysis and comparison of the words modifying the word 'hand' between the two novels demonstrates Dickens's creative use of body language and the change of his style in describing the characters.

The collocations I deal with are in the construction: [(determiner +) modifiers + 'hand']. In the following two tables, the collocations are shown individually for each character. In Table 3, the collocations for four main characters of *Oliver Twist* are listed. In Table 4, the collocations for five main characters of *A Tale of Two Cities* are divided into two columns: E and F. The instances in E indicate that they occur in the English scenes and those in F, in the French scenes.

The total number of words in *Oliver Twist* is approximately 160,000, and examples of the word 'hand' are found 342 times. The novel *A Tale of Two Cities* includes approximately 140,000 words along with 370 instances of 'hand.' The different word frequencies between the two works are not significant.

Furthermore, such instances in bold as 'his stiffening hand' applied to Fagin and 'her appealing hands' given to Lucie are only used to describe the characters in the *Dickens Corpus*.[5] To put it another way, those expressions only occur with reference to a particular character in Dickens's 23 works.

Table 3. Collocations of 'modifiers + hand' in *OT*

Oliver	his little hands (3) / his other hand (4) / his unoccupied hand (4) / a trembling hand (5) / his little withered hand (12) / Oliver's unoccupied hand (16) / his other hand (22) / his trembling hand (33) / his folded hands (51) / the disengaged hand (52)
Fagin	his skinny hands (19) / his right hand (20) / his clenched hand (17) / his right hand (43) / his bony hands (44) / his other hand (47) / his right hand (twice) (47)

---

[5] In fact, the use of the word 'stiffening' can be observed in the three corpora, but the combination 'stiffening hand' cannot be found except in this instance.

114

Sikes	his other hand (15) / Sikes's heavy hand (39) / his heavy hand (47) / his huge hand (47) / his **stiffening hand** (50)
Nancy	the young lady's right hand (15) / both hands (44) / her folded hands (47)

Note. The numerals in parentheses of each instance refer to the chapter in which the expression is used.

Table 4. Collocations of 'modifiers + hand' in *TTC*

Lucie	E	the hesitating little hand (I, 4) / 'her cold hands' (I, 4) / delicate hands (II, 6) / her agitated hand (II, 18)
	F	her **appealing hands** (I.6) / her **appealing hand** (III, 3)
Dr. Manette	E	**emaciated** hands (I, 3) / 'this honoured hand' (II, 10) / his two hands (twice) (II, 10) / his own hand (II, 18)
	F	the right hand (I, 6) / the left hand (I, 6) / 'this **gaunt hand**' (III, 10) / 'my own hands' (III, 10)
Mr. Lorry	E	his left hand (twice) (I, 4) / both hands (I, 4)
	F	the clasping hand (III, 2) / his troubled hand (III, 8)
Carton	F	his open hand (III, 8) / his **eager but so firm and steady hand** (III, 12) / his right hand (III, 13) / 'your **brave hand**' (III, 13)
Madame Defarge	F	a large hand (I, 5) / her left hand (I, 5) / her right hand (II, 16) / her extended hand (II, 16) / Madame's **resolute right** hand (II, 21) / 'these two hands' (III, 12) / The two hands (III, 14)

Analysis of the two tables above allows for the following observations.

First, as a feature common to the two novels, Dickens frequently uses adjectives to describe visual characteristics of a character's 'hand.' For example, the expressions 'his little hands' and 'his unoccupied hand' given to Oliver, 'his skinny hands' and 'his bony hands' to Fagin, 'a large hand' and 'her extended hand' to Madame Defarge, and 'emaciated hands' and 'the right hand' to Dr. Manette represent the external appearance of each character's 'hand.'

Second, when such collocations in Table 4 as Lucie's 'agitated hand,' Mr. Lorry's 'troubled hand,' and Carton's 'brave hand' are closely examined, we notice that modifiers denoting human tendencies like fear and confidence, so-called transferred epithets, more frequently co-occur with the characters' 'hand' in *A Tale of Two Cities* compared with *Oliver*

Twist. In other words, the collocations including transferred epithets are more frequently utilized to indicate the characters' attitudes and states of mind in context in the later novel.

Third, the descriptions of the outward appearances of the characters' 'hand' are used for psychological characterization. To take a typical example, the transferred epithet 'appealing' in Lucie's 'appealing hand' in Table 4 appropriately depicts her psychological state of calling for help as shown in quotation (2) below. Lucie has a compassionate nature and the power to inspire great love and peace of mind in other characters, but she does not play an active role by herself. The people surrounding her, such as Mr. Lorry and Sydney Carton, draw their strength from her and act on her behalf. Each instance of 'her appealing hand' situationally represents Lucie's attitudes and states of mind in context, and at the same time, suggests her role in the novel.[6]

(2)   But, the suppressed manner had enough of menace in it—not visible and presented, but indistinct and withheld—to alarm Lucie into saying, as she laid *her appealing hand* on Madame Defarge's dress:
        'You will be good to my poor husband. You will do him no harm. You will help me to see him if you can?' (*TTC* III.3)

Fourth, the difference in use of synonymous adjectives between the two works shows one of Dickens's creative uses of body language. In Table 3, the descriptive adjectives 'skinny' and 'bony' are used to describe Fagin's hands which are very thin. It is needless to say that these adjectives are also employed to describe Dickens's other characters' hands in his other works: Uriah's 'bony hands' in *David Copperfield* (1849–50) and Mrs. Brown's 'skinny hands' in *Dombey and Son* (1846–8).

On the other hand, in Table 4, we can see the adjectives 'emaciated' and 'gaunt' in the descriptions of Dr. Manette's very thin hands.[7] According to the *OED2*, the word 'emaciated' is of Latin origin, and the origin of the adjective 'gaunt' is not clearly defined. The combination 'gaunt hand' is

---

[6] Italicized and underlined words are my own, unless otherwise indicated.
[7] The *OED2* defines the origin of the verb 'emaciate' as follows: f. L. ēmaciāt- ppl. stem of ēmaciāre + ē out + maci-es leanness, and 'gaunt' in this manner: of unknown origin.

only observed in the descriptions of Dr. Manette's hand, and is not found elsewhere in the *Dickens Corpus*, the *19th Works Corpus*, or the *18th Works Corpus*. It can be said to be a kind of unusual collocation. The use of these adjectives is closely related to the characterization of Dr. Manette, who is a French physician, and has an unusual experience of being imprisoned in the Bastille for 18 years because of his knowledge of the evil doings of the French aristocrats. Dickens tactfully uses different synonymous adjectives and their collocates specifically for each character and each work in the elaborate scheme of creating his characters.

Fifth, the numbers of the instances in bold, which only occur with reference to a single character in Dickens's 23 works, are quite different between the two tables, or between the two novels. We can see such instances more frequently in Table 4 than Table 3. In other words, it seems that Dickens exploits the collocations that are unique to a certain character distinctive of other characters more often in the later work, compared to his earlier novel.

Brook (1970: 21) acutely points out Dickens's use of adjectives as follows:

(3) One feature of Dickens's style . . . is his readiness to use adjectives freely. As we have seen, the adjectives are often conventional, adding little to a description that a reader could not have imagined for himself, but they are sometimes very effective, giving a life-like picture in a very concise way.

In addition to the skillful exploitation of the transferred epithets and the different synonymous adjectives, the example 'his eager but so firm and steady hand' applied to Carton in Table 4 represents how Dickens is willing to employ multiple modifiers, with the conjunctions 'but' and 'and,' to describe his hero's hand. This fact is not only closely related to his characterization but also to the subject matter of *A Tale of Two Cities*. This point will be discussed in detail later in this paper.

4. Combinations of 'verbs + hand'

Here, my attention is turned to the combination of 'verbs + hand,' especially the construction 'rub one's hands.'

Passage (4) below is quoted from the *Dickens Lexicon Digital*, which is a compilation of approximately 60,000 entries painstakingly drawn up by Dr. Tadao Yamamoto (1904–91)[8] and is expected to be released on an internet website in the near future. Moreover, quotation (5) is a passage from *Our Mutual Friend* (1864–5) in which we can see the example of the cluster 'rub one's nose' as Yamamoto, in fact, notes.

(4) The nose is rubbed when one is vexed or perplexed in thought. Examples are not rare in Dickens. (*DLD*, s.v. rub one's nose)

(5) 'Never was an obstinate person yet, who would own to the word!' remarked Miss Potterson, *rubbing her vexed nose*; 'I'm sure I would, if I was obstinate; but I am a pepperer, which is different. Lizzie Hexam, Lizzie Hexam, think again. Do you know the worst of your father?' (*OMF* I, 6)

Yamamoto points out Dickens's frequent use of the expression 'rub one's nose' in describing his characters' body actions.   In fact, in the *Dickens Corpus*, 35 instances with the construction can be found, while on the other hand, in the *19th Works Corpus*, only four instances by three authors are present, and no examples in the *18th Works Corpus*. This fact exposes Dickens's preference for the action of 'rubbing one's nose' in the descriptions of his characters.

Dickens's predilection for the expression 'rubbing one's nose' seems to reveal one of his stylistic features in the use of body language, but I cannot pursue this matter at this point. To do so would carry us too far away from the purpose of the present paper. Instead, my attention is devoted to the combination 'rub one's hands.' Before examining the object of my interest carefully, I will investigate what verbs are frequently connected with 'hand' as their object. Table 5 below shows the 20 highest-frequency occurrences of verbs in the construction 'verbs + hand' among the three different corpora. Here again, since the three corpora have differing amounts of words, the table shows normalized frequencies per million words for comparison.

---

[8] Partial results of his laborious research are contained in his admirable book *Growth and System of the Language of Dickens* (1950 [2003]).

118

Table 5. Frequencies of 'verbs + hand' among the three corpora

	Dickens Corpus App. 4,499,000 words			19th Works Corpus App. 13,534,000 words			18th Works Corpus App. 5,111,000 words		
R.	Word	Freq	/1M	Word	Freq	/1M	Word	Freq	/1M
1	put	385	85.6	put	692	51.1	take	145	28.4
2	shake	333	74.0	take	554	40.9	lay	118	23.1
3	lay	314	69.8	hold	506	37.4	kiss	92	18.0
4	rub	170	37.8	lay	325	24.0	hold	84	16.4
5	take	148	32.9	shake	271	20.0	give	80	15.7
6	hold	145	32.2	give	259	19.1	put	71	13.9
7	give	134	29.8	press	166	12.3	lift	64	12.5
8	clasp	118	26.2	kiss	162	12.0	wring	45	8.8
9	clap	90	20.0	clasp	134	9.9	clap	28	5.5
10	kiss	89	19.8	stretch	118	8.7	snatch	26	5.1
11	wave	86	19.1	lift	113	8.3	seize	23	4.5
12	press	75	16.7	wave	104	7.7	press	20	3.9
13	wring	70	15.6	offer	100	7.4	clasp	18	3.5
14	stretch	69	15.3	raise	92	6.8	withdraw	18	3.5
15	fold	62	13.8	rub	84	6.2	rub	14	2.7
16	raise	54	12.0	pass	82	6.1	keep	13	2.5
17	pass	50	11.1	keep	80	5.9	wave	13	2.5
18	thrust	44	9.8	seize	66	4.9	get	12	2.3
19	draw	38	8.4	clap	64	4.7	thrust	11	2.2
20	grasp	34	7.6	wring	59	4.4	grasp	11	2.2

A quick glance at Table 5 shows that the verbs listed in the *Dickens Corpus* and the *19th Works Corpus* columns are relatively similar in type and in rank order, compared to the *18th Works Corpus*. A comparison of raw figures and figures normalized per one million words among the three corpora demonstrates that the number of instances increases in 19th-century works, compared to works in the 18th century, and furthermore significantly increases in Dickens's works.

Now, I first compare the verbs listed in the table between the *Dickens Corpus* and the *19th Works Corpus*. The highest-frequency item is the verb 'put,' and in total sixteen of the 20 verbs are listed in both corpora with slightly different ranks: that is to say, 14 verbs from the verb 'put' at Rank 1 to 'stretch' at Rank 14, and two more verbs, 'raise' at Rank 16 and 'pass' at Rank 17 in the *Dickens Corpus,* are in common with the *19th*

Works Corpus. Roughly speaking, both corpora indicate a similar tendency in types of verbs in the combination 'verbs + hand,' even though Dickens tends to use the combination more frequently. However, the greatest distinction between the two corpora is the frequency of the verb 'rub.' In the *Dickens Corpus* it is at Rank 8 with 37.8 instances as a normalized figure per one million words, while in the *19th Works Corpus*, it is at Rank 15 with 6.2 instances as a normalized figure. The collocation of 'rub one's hands' does not simply suggest Dickens's idiosyncratic style, but the discrepancy in frequency reveals the author's strong preference for the expression in the descriptions of his characters' body actions, as observed in the frequent use of the cluster 'rub one's nose,' compared to other authors of the 19th century.

Moreover, a comparison of the verbs between the *Dickens Corpus* and the *18th Works Corpus* shows that fourteen of the 20 verbs are listed in common in the two corpora, even though the rank orders of the verbs are slightly different. The verb 'put,' which ranks first in the *Dickens Corpus* and the *19th Works Corpus*, is at Rank 6, and the verb 'rub' is at Rank 15 with 14 examples as raw figure and 2.7 instances as normalized figure in the *18th Works Corpus*. The verb 'rub' is ranked at the same rank order in the *18th Works Corpus* and the *19th Works Corpus*. Actually, the collocation of 'rub one's hands' is less frequently seen in the *18th Works Corpus* in normalized frequencies per million words.

Next, I focus my attention on how Dickens uses the collocation 'rub one's hands' in the creation of his characters.

Table 6 below shows frequencies of the construction of 'rub one's hands' in Dickens's works.

Table 6. Frequencies of 'rub one's hands' in Dickens's works

	Works	Tokens	Freq.	/1M
1	*Nicholas Nickleby*	328,963	27	82.1
2	*Martin Chuzzlewit*	344,004	21	61.0
3	*Dombey and Son*	349,157	21	60.1
4	*Pickwick Papers*	308,775	18	58.3
5	*Old Curiosity Shop*	221,846	14	63.1
6	*David Copperfield*	362,866	11	30.3
7	*Oliver Twist*	161,366	10	62.0

8	*Barnaby Rudge*	258,579	10	38.7
9	*Bleak House*	361,136	8	22.2
10	*Sketches by Boz*	198,604	6	30.2
11	*Our Mutual Friend*	332,912	6	18.0
12	*Little Dorrit*	344,216	5	14.5
13	*Great Expectations*	188,546	5	26.5
14	*Reprinted Pieces*	93,685	3	32.0
15	*A Christmas Carol*	29,200	2	68.5
16	*Battle of Life*	30,664	1	32.6
17	*A Tale of Two Cities*	138,138	1	7.2
18	*Haunted Man*	34,907	1	28.6

An analysis of Table 6 illustrates that the cluster of 'rub one's hands' is used across 18 of Dickens's 23 works, and that it is most frequently employed in *Nicholas Nickleby* (1838–9) according to raw figures and figures normalized per one million words. In fact, in this work, the combination can be observed in the descriptions of more than ten characters, such as Arthur Gride (4 times), Mrs. Nickleby (twice), Miss La Creevy (twice), and Mr. Cheeryble (twice). Moreover, in *Dombey and Son*, this distinctive example of body language can be also found in the depictions of more than ten characters, with seven of 21 instances given to Solomon Gills. This means that the body action of 'rubbing one's hands' is repeatedly employed across texts to describe Dickens's characters reflective of the body language of real people, and that in some works the expression is deliberately and recurrently used to depict some particular characters in his works.

Here, my attention is devoted to the use of the body language of 'rubbing one's hands' in *Oliver Twist*, which includes 10 instances of the expression with a normalized frequency of 62.0. Table 7 below shows a concordance for 'hand' with the verb 'rub.' In the table, such items in bold as 'the Jew' (5 times), 'The old man' (once), 'Fagin' (twice), and the personal pronoun 'he' (once) refer back to the same character, that is to say, Fagin. This shows that nine of 10 instances of 'rub one's hands', with the exception of item 5 in Table 7, are utilized to describe Fagin's body language, and that the expression helps to individualize and highlight this particular person, conveying his 'relatively stable mental conditions (such as […] opinions, values, personality traits,' as one function of body language or 'externalisers' according to Korte (1997: 41).

Table 7. Use of 'rub one's hands' in *OT*

1	expressive look; 'that's why.' **The Jew**	rubbed his hands; and, sitting down at
2	my dear, such plate!' said **the Jew**:	rubbing his hands, and elevating his
3	cool for the time of year,' said **Fagin**,	rubbing his hands. 'From the country,
4	catechism of his trade.' **The old man**	rubbed his hands gleefully together, as
5	be sure, so he will,' repeated Charley,	rubbing his hands. 'I think I see him
6	'em. Ha! ha!' chuckled **the Jew**,	rubbing his hands, 'it couldn't have
7	good indeed, my dear!' said **the Jew**,	rubbing his hands. 'Oh, my brother!
8	length **he** made another attempt; and	rubbing his hands together, said, in
9	you're a brave boy, Oliver.' **The Jew**	rubbed his hands with a chuckle, but
10	moment's hesitation. 'Ah!' said **Fagin**,	rubbing his hands with great satisfaction

Before I examine how Fagin is described through the action of 'rubbing his hands,' I will look at the definition of the expression in the *OED2*.

(6) Definition of 'to rub hands' in the *OED2*
   1.c To make (one's hands) move over and press upon each other, as a sign of satisfaction. Also *fig.*
   1778 F. Burney *Evelina* lxxxii, [He] *rubbed his hands*, and was scarce able to contain the fullness of his glee. **1831** Scott *Ct. Rob. vi*, He sighed and *rubbed his hands* with pleasure, like a man newly restored to liberty.

According to the *OED2*, as seen in quotation (5), the action of rubbing one's hands is defined 'as a sign of satisfaction.' In fact, in the two examples quoted in the *OED2*, which are from the works of Burney and Scott, the expression 'rubbed his hands' co-occurs with the underlined phrases 'the fullness of his glee' and 'with pleasure,' both of which indicate some satisfaction derived by the agents of the action.

In addition to the definition above, Kobayashi (1991: 419–20) points out that the body language of 'rubbing one's hands' denotes not only 'a sign of satisfaction' but also the person's obsequious attitude or his or her insinuative action.

122

Now, I investigate how the expression of 'rub his hands' characterizes Fagin in two quotations as follows.

(7) Description of Fagin in *OT*
> 'Tush, tush, my dear!' said the Jew, abruptly resuming his old manner, and playing with the knife a little, before he laid it down; as if to induce the belief that he had caught it up, in mere sport. 'Of course I know that, my dear. I only tried to frighten you. You're a brave boy. Ha! ha! you're a brave boy, Oliver.' The Jew **rubbed his hands** with a chuckle, but glanced uneasily at the box, notwithstanding.
> 'Did you see any of these pretty things, my dear?' said the Jew, laying his hand upon it after a short pause. (Ch. 9)

Here, Fagin is worried about the discovery that Oliver was watching him gloating over a box full of jewelry and watches. He takes hold of a bread knife and asks Oliver if he was awake an hour before. Oliver says he was not. Fagin regains his genial manner, and explains that the treasure is a little savings for his old age.

Fagin's body language of 'rubbing his hands,' along with the phrase 'with a chuckle,' indicates his ostensible cheerfulness, and contributes to the concealment of his own true thoughts. However, in fact, the co-occurrence of the underlined expression 'glanced uneasily at the box' reveals the great anxiety in his mind. The co-existence of the action of rubbing his hands with the phrase expressive of his real state of mind exposes his real traits as a two-faced hypocrite. He apparently shows a trace of kindness to Oliver, but in fact he tries to make a pickpocket out of the boy. Behind his facade of benevolence he hides a cruel nature.

A similar thing can be seen in the following quotation:

(8) Description of Fagin in *OT*
> During the silence, the Jew looked restlessly about the room, as if to assure himself that there were no appearances of Sikes having covertly returned. Apparently satisfied with his inspection, he coughed twice or thrice, and made as many efforts to open a conversation; but the girl heeded him no more than if he had been made of stone. At length he made another attempt; and **rubbing his hands** together, said, in his most conciliatory tone,
> 'And where should you think Bill was now, my dear?' (Ch. 26)

Passage (8) appears in the context where Fagin goes to Bill Sikes's lodgings, where he displays a cheery mood and asks Nancy about Sikes. The body language of 'rubbing his hands' represents his 'conciliatory' gesture toward her, while the underlined sentence 'the Jew looked restlessly about the room' indicates his resourceful cunning. The repeated use of body language in the descriptions of Fagin reveals the discrepancy between his appearance and his real self, and contributes to the creation of 'one of Dickens' few truly great villains' (Mono 1968: 132). In short, particular emphasis is given to the body action of 'rubbing his hands,' which Mahlberg (2014: 386) calls a 'highlighting function': 'body language that is habitual or so striking that it is an identifying feature of a specific fictional character.'

Furthermore, the body language of 'rubbing one's hands' leads itself not only to the individualization of characters but also to irony. Observe the following passage from *David Copperfield* (1849–50) as a typical example.

(9) Description of Mrs. Crupp in *DC*
 Mrs. Crupp, who had been incessantly smiling to express sweet temper, and incessantly holding her head on one side, to express a general feebleness of constitution, and incessantly ***rubbing her hands***, to express a desire to be of service to all deserving objects, gradually smiled herself, one-sided herself, and ***rubbed herself***, out of the room. 'Dick!' said my aunt. 'You know what I told you about time-servers and wealth-worshippers?' (Ch. 34)

Here, David warmly welcomes Miss Trotwood and Mr. Dick, who have suddenly visited him, with spontaneous affection. Mrs. Crupp, who is the landlady of the apartment building where David rents rooms, offers too great a sense of hospitality to his visitors. However, her hospitality is intentional and outward, which is revealed through the two kinds of repeated constructions 'incessantly + verb of present participle + to express + objects' and 'verb of past tense + herself.' The bodily action of 'rubbing' is employed in both constructions for visually depicting one of Mrs. Crupp's servile actions to ingratiate herself with Miss Trotwood.

In the first repeated construction, Mrs. Crupp's incessant 'rubbing her hands' expresses her wicked and treacly 'desire to be of service to' David's rich relations. Moreover, in the second iterative construction, her

124

overdramatic action of going out of David's room is described in a sequence of such exaggerated expressions as 'smiled herself,' 'one-sided herself,'[9] and 'rubbed herself,' which is end-focused. The repetitive use of the body language of rubbing, with the help of other body actions, leads the reader to notice Dickens's ironical attitude toward Mrs. Crupp as the vey archetype of 'time-servers and wealth-worshippers.'

Moreover, the body language of 'rubbing one's hands' is also utilized for reflecting a character's state of mind.

(10) Description of David's action of 'rubbing' in *DC*

But in the course of the evening I had rambled down to the door, and a little way along the street, that I might have another peep at the old houses, and the grey Cathedral; and might think of my coming through that old city on my journey, and of my passing the very house I lived in, without knowing it. As I came back, I saw Uriah Heep shutting up the office; and feeling friendly towards everybody, went in and spoke to him, and at parting, gave him my hand. But oh, what a clammy hand his was! as ghostly to the touch as to the sight! *I rubbed mine* afterwards, to warm it, AND *TO RUB HIS OFF*. (Ch. 15)

In the context of passage (9), David comes back after the short walk, and unexpectedly encounters Uriah Heep, who works as a clerk in Mr. Wickfield's law office and has a 'long, lean, and skeleton' hand. Uriah hides behind a facade of humility. His cant of humility and his sliminess so disgust David that he feels the need to rub off Uriah's touch after shaking his hand. His action of rubbing his hands, which is depicted as 'I rubbed mine,' reflects his hatred for Uriah, and seems to convey his temporary emotional or psychological state in this scene, that is to say, his 'emotional display' according to Korte (1997: 40).

The conspicuous gesture of 'rubbing one's hands,' as one of Dickens's favorites, is repeatedly applied to peculiar characters in texts for characterization and character identification, revealing characters' states of mind, and furthermore contributing to the creation of the author's ironical attitude.

---

[9] This is an example of a back formation from 'one-sided.' See Yamamoto (1950 [2003]: 315).

5. Body Language as a means of dramatization

In this section, my attention is focused on body language as a means of dramatization in that it 'helps to illustrate a fictional event, to make it more scenic, concrete, and vivid' (Korte 1997: 146–7). In other words, the repetitive use of expressions, including the body part noun 'hand,' serves to make a scene visually conspicuous, and in some cases suggests a key theme of a work.

Brook (1970: 36) points out that 'Dickens was never afraid of making excessive use of a way of writing that happened to appeal to him.' Furthermore, as to the functions of the 'hand,' compared to those of the 'head' or 'eye,' Mahlberg (2013: 108) states as follows:

(11) Body parts differ in their potential of expression because of their physical conditions. Hands are very flexible and the head and eyes prominent with eyes specifically being able to convey a variety of emotions.

The repetitive use of such expressions, including the bodily word 'hand' with its characteristic feature of flexible movement, serves to make a scene more dramatic. Let us observe one typical example from *A Tale of Two Cities*. In this work, the word 'hand' is repetitively used in the descriptions of most of the characters, with higher frequencies of the word assigned to Dr. Manette, Lucie, and Sydney Carton. Here, I examine the creative use of body language in the descriptions of Carton's 'hand.'

Carton's 'hand' occurs 38 times, and Table 8 below demonstrates how the 38 instances are distributed among chapters.

Table 8. Distribution of Carton's 'hand'

Chap.	English Chapters					French Chapters				
	II, 2	II, 3	II, 5	II, 13	II, 20	III, 8	III, 9	III, 12	III, 13	III, 14
Freq.	1	1	4	1	1	3	2	2	20	3

Table 8 illustrates that Carton's 'hand' is present most frequently in Chapter 13 of Book III (21 out of 38, 55%). In this chapter, Carton causes Darnay to slip into unconsciousness and substitutes himself for him in prison. The very frequent and intensive references to his 'hand' in this

126

chapter bring his heroic self-sacrifice to the foreground. More concretely, the process of Carton's action of drugging Darnay is depicted through repeated references to his 'hand,' which is reiterated as many as 11 times within three pages.[10] This series of repetitions is presented as follows:

(12) Carton, with *his right hand* in his breast, stood close beside him.
(13) Carton still had *his hand* in his breast.
(14) Carton, standing over him with *his hand* in his breast, looked down.
(15) He was drawing *his hand* from his breast; . . . .
(16) . . . *the hand* stopped, closing upon something.
(17) . . . *his hand* slowly and softly moved down close to the writer's face.
(18) . . . Carton—*his hand* again in his breast—looked steadily at him.
(19) . . . *Carton's hand* was again watchfully and softly stealing down; . . . .
(20) . . . *the hand* was at the prisoner's face; . . . .
(21) *Carton's hand* moved back to his breast no more.
(22) . . . *Carton's hand* was close and firm at his nostrils, ...

In this scene, the repeated combination of 'his (right) hand' with 'in his breast' (from (12) to (14)) suggests Carton's waiting for the opportunity to take out a sleeping drug. The initiating action is represented in (15) with the combination 'drawing his hand' with 'from his breast.' From (16) to (22) (excluding (18)), the action of Carton's drugging Darnay is vividly described through the repetitive construction [Carton's 'hand' + predicate verb]. In this way, Dickens makes a graphic description of Carton's heroic conduct.

Additionally, the arrangement of the combinations of his 'hand' with modifiers attracts my attention. The combination 'his eager but so firm and steady hand' occurs at the end of Chapter 12 of Book III just before Carton tries to take Darnay's place in the prison in Chapter 13 of Book III, as can be observed in quotation (23) below. The transferred epithets 'eager,' 'firm,' and 'steady' in the combination represent Carton's positive features, which have not been mentioned by the novelist before. The combination does not directly foreshadow Carton's heroic act of

---

[10] In Chapter 13 of Book III in *A Tale of Two Cities*, the word 'hand' occurs 31 times in total. Twenty of the 31 instances are given to descriptions of Carton's 'hand.'

self-devotion, but leads the reader to expect his unprecedented action in the following scene.

(23)   'You have my certificate in your hand with the rest, you know, and will reserve my place. Wait for nothing but to have my place occupied, and then for England!'

'Why, then,' said Mr. Lorry, grasping *his eager but so firm and steady hand*, 'it does not all depend on one old man, but I shall have a young and ardent man at my side.'

'By the help of Heaven you shall! Promise me solemnly that nothing will influence you to alter the course on which we now stand pledged to one another.'

'Nothing, Carton.' (*TTC* III, 12)

Furthermore, in the following scene of Chapter 13 of Book III, that is to say, in quotation (24) below, a seamstress and Sydney Carton travel in the tumbrel to the guillotine.

(24)   'I heard you were released, Citizen Evremonde. I hoped it was true?' 'It was. But, I was again taken and condemned.'

'If I may ride with you, Citizen Evremonde, will you *let me hold your hand*? I am not afraid, but I am little and weak, and it will give me more courage.'

As the patient eyes were lifted to his face, he saw a sudden doubt in them, and then astonishment. He pressed the work-worn, hunger-worn young fingers, and touched his lips.

'Are you dying for him?' she whispered.

'And his wife and child. Hush! Yes.'

'O you will *let me hold your brave hand*, stranger?' (*TTC* III, 14)

The seamstress first thinks that the person executed with her is Charles Darnay, or Citizen Evremonde, and asks for his permission for her to hold his hand. After a short while, she realizes that the person is not Darnay, and that he sacrifices himself for Darnay, and Darnay's wife and child. She reiterates her desire to hold Carton's 'brave hand.' The combination 'brave + hand' is peculiar to Carton, which means that any other example of the cluster cannot be found, at least in the three corpora examined in the present paper. Such an unusual collocation serves to catch the reader's eye. As a result, through the iterative use of the construction [Carton's 'hand' + predicate verb] and two unusual collocations 'his eager but so firm and steady hand' and 'his brave hand,' Carton is brought into the foreground, and thus his heroic self-sacrifice is dramatized as the plot develops to the climax.[11]

6. Final Remarks

The foregoing arguments, though tentative and limited, have focused on body language, especially on the bodily part of the 'hand.' This examination clearly supports the assertion that body language was widely used in 19th-century works and that, above all, Dickens deliberately exploits the 'hand' with great artistry in order to individualize characters, to indicate the characters' states of mind, to make a scene more dramatic, and to convey the dominant themes of the novel to the reader. Furthermore, he carries out these literary strategies more intensely and consistently than other major writers of the 18th and 19th century.

My research, with special reference to Dickens's stylistic use of body language, which is partly embodied in the employment of the word 'hand,' serves to reveal the writer's stylistic and linguistic artistry that inheres, with some qualitative alternations and transformations, through-out his works. Such an approach undoubtedly throws light on the system and structure of Dickens's language, which represents in many ways the fullest maturity of English prose.

The next task will be to make more extensive and exhaustive observations of the body language in Dickens's works through the conducting of quantitative and qualitative analyses of other body part nouns, such as 'eye,' 'face,' 'nose,' and 'head.'

---

[11] Dickens demonstrates that the seamstress is society's innocent victim, a sacrificial heroine both before and during the Revolution through the unusual collocation 'the work-worn, hunger-worn young fingers.'

References

Brook, G. Leslie. 1970. *The language of Dickens*. London: André Deutsch.

Carter, Ronald. 1998. *Vocabulary: Applied linguistic perspectives* 2nd edition. London: Routledge.

Connor, Steven. 1985. *Charles Dickens*. Oxford: Basil Blackwell.

Fowler, Roger. 1977. *Linguistics and the novel*. London: Methuen.

Glancy, Ruth. 1991. *A Tale of Two Cities: Dickens's revolutionary novel*. Boston: Twayne Publishers.

Gliserman, Martin. 1996. *Psychoanalysis, language and the body of the text*. Florida: University Press of Florida.

Hori, Masahiro. 2004. *Investigating Dickens' style: A collocational analysis*. New York: Palgrave Macmillan.

Imahayashi, Osamu. 2006. *Charles Dickens and literary dialect*. Hiroshima: Keisuisha.

Imai, Mitsunori. 2004. Repetition in Middle English Metrical Romances. In Risto Hiltunen & Shinichiro Watanabe (eds.), *Approaches to style and discourse in English*, 27–50. Osaka: Osaka University Press.

Kobayashi, Yuko. 1991. *Shigusa no eigo hyogen jiten* [A dictionary of gestures and expressions in English]. Tokyo: Kenkyusha.

Koguchi, Keisuke. 2009. *Repetition in Dickens's* A Tale of Two Cities*: An exploration into his linguistic artistry*. Hiroshima: Keisuisha.

Korte, Barbara. 1997. *Body language in literature*. Toronto: University of Toronto Press.

Leech, Geoffrey & Mick Short. 2007. *Style in fiction: A linguistic introduction to English fictional prose* 2nd edition. London: Longman.

Mahlberg, Michaela. 2013. *Corpus stylistics and Dickens's fiction*. New York: Routledge.

_____. 2014. Corpus stylistics. In Burke, M. (ed.), *The Routledge handbook of stylistics*, 378–92. London: Routledge.

McMaster, Juliet. 1987. *Dickens the designer*. New Jersey: Barnes & Noble Books.

Monod, Sylvere. 1968. *Dickens the novelist*. Norman: University of Oklahoma Press.

Page, Norman. 1988. *Speech in the English novel* 2nd edition. London: Macmillan.

Quirk, Randolph. 1974. *The linguist and the English language*. London: Edward Arnold.

130

Sørensen, Knud. 1985. *Charles Dickens: Linguistic innovator*. Aarhus: Arkona.
Yamamoto, Tadao. 1950 (2003). *Growth and system of the language of Dickens: An introduction to A Dickens lexicon* 3rd edition. Hiroshima: Keisuisha.

Appendix

The *Dickens Corpus*:
Sketches by Boz (1833–6), *The Pickwick Papers* (1836–7), *Oliver Twist* (1837–9), *Nicholas Nickleby* (1838–9), *The Old Curiosity Shop* (1840–1), *Barnaby Rudge* (1841), *A Christmas Carol* (1843), *Martin Chuzzlewit* (1843–4), *The Chimes* (1844), *The Cricket on the Hearth* (1845), *The Battle of Life* (1846), *Dombey and Son* (1846–8), *The Haunted Man* (1848), *David Copperfield* (1849–50), *Reprinted Pieces* (1850-6), *Bleak House* (1852–3), *Hard Times* (1854), *Little Dorrit* (1855–7), *A Tale of Two Cities* (1859), *The Uncommercial Traveller* (1860), *Great Expectations* (1860–61), *Our Mutual Friend* (1864–5), *The Mystery of Edwin Drood* (1869–70).

The *19th Works Corpus*:
Austen, *Sense and Sensibility* (1811), *Pride and Prejudice* (1813), *Mansfield Park* (1814), *Emma* (1815), *Northanger Abbey* (1817), *Persuasion* (1817); C. Brontë, *Jane Eyre* (1847), *Shirley* (1849), *Villette* (1853), *The Professor* (1857); E. Brontë, *Wuthering Heights* (1847), Carroll, *Alice's Adventures in Wonderland* (1865), *Through the Looking-Glass* (1871); Collins, *The Woman in White* (1860), *No Name* (1862), *Armadale* (1866), *The Moonstone* (1868), *Man and Wife* (1870); Eliot, *Scenes of Clerical Life* (1857), *Adam Bede* (1859), *The Mill on the Floss* (1860), *Silas Marner* (1861), *Romola* (1863), *Felix Holt, the Radical* (1866), *Middlemarch* (1871–2), *Daniel Deronda* (1876); Gaskell, *Sylvia's Lovers* (1863), *Wives and Daughters* (1864); Gissing, *The Nether World* (1889), *New Grub Street* (1891), *The Odd Women* (1893), *The Whirlpool* (1897); Hardy, *A Pair of Blue Eyes* (1872), *Far from the Madding Crowd* (1874), *The Return of the Native* (1878), *The Trumpet-Major* (1880), *The Woodlanders* (1887), *Tess of the d'Urbervilles* (1891), *The Well-Beloved* (1897), *Jude the Obscure* (1895); Scott, *Waverley* (1814), *Guy Mannering* (1815), *The Antiquary* (1816), *The Black Dwarf* (1816), *The Heart of Midlothian* (1818), *A Legend of Montrose* (1819), *Ivanhoe* (1819), *The Bride of Lammermoor* (1819), *Kenilworth* (1821), *Quentin Durward* (1823), *Saint Ronan's Well* (1823), *Redgauntlet* (1824); Stevenson, *Treasure Island* (1883), *Dr. Jekyll and Mr. Hyde* (1886), *Weir of Hermiston* (1896);

Thackeray, *Catherine* (1839–40), *Barry Lyndon* (1844), *Vanity Fair* (1847–8), *Pendennis* (1850), *Henry Esmond* (1852), *The Newcomes* (1855), *Rebecca and Rowena* (1856), *The Virginians* (1857–9); Trollope, *The Warden* (1855), *Barchester Towers* (1857), *Doctor Thorne* (1858), *Framley Parsonage* (1861), *The Small House at Allington* (1864), *Can You Forgive Her?* (1864), *The Last Chronicle of Barset* (1867), *Phineas Finn* (1869), *The Eustace Diamonds* (1873), *Phineas Redux* (1873), *The Prime Minister* (1876).

The *18th Works Corpus*:
Brooke, *The History of Emily Montague* (1769); Burney, *Evelina* (1778); Defoe, *Robinson Crusoe* (1719), *Captain Singleton* (1720), *Moll Flanders* (1722), *Colonel Jack* (1722), *A Journal of the Plague Year* (1722), *Military Memoirs of Capt. George Carleton* (1728); Fielding, *Joseph Andrews* (1742), *Jonathan Wild* (1743), *Tom Jones* (1749), *A Journey from this World to the Next* (1749), *Amelia* (1751); Goldsmith, *The Vicar of Wakefield* (1766); Haywood, *The Fortunate Foundlings* (1744), *Life's Progress through the Passions* (1748), *The History of Miss Betsy Thoughtless* (1751); Richardson, *Pamela* (1740), *Clarissa* (1748); Smollett, *Ferdinand Count Fathom* (1753), *Humphry Clinker* (1771), *Sir Launcelot Greaves* (1762), *Roderick Random* (1748), *Peregrine Pickle* (1751), *Travels through France and Italy* (1766); Sterne, *Tristram Shandy* (1759), *A Political Romance* (1759), *A Sentimental Journey through France and Italy* (1768); Swift, *A Tale of a Tub* (1704), *Gulliver's Travels* (1726), *A Journal to Stella* (1766)

Facial Expressions and Eye Behavior in American Literature: A Case Study of Ernest Hemingway's *The Sun Also Rises*

Hirotoshi Takeshita

1. Introduction

Body language as non-verbal communication in literature never fails to play an important part in adding depth to the descriptions of characters in literary works. The research in this paper is part of an ongoing attempt to unveil several aspects of such body language in American literature in terms of change and development of literary style. Accordingly, my immediate purpose is to shed light on a part of body language employed by Ernest Hemingway, one of the most influential authors in 20th-century American literature, and to examine how it works with his 'hard-boiled' style through a comparison of his novels and short stories with those of some other prominent American authors.

In his suggestive article, Eschholz (1973) refers to Mark Twain, whose *Adventures of Huckleberry Finn* (1885), as is well known, exerted a significant degree of influence on Hemingway's literary style:

(1)   Mark Twain's use of the language of gesture reveals a new aspect of his
       genius. [. . .] His knowledge of the language of gesture serves to enrich his
       work. Body language not only is more focused and succinct than often
       cumbersome dialogue, but also leaves an unmistakable or indelible
       impression of particular characters with the reader. In addition, it can function
       thematically as it does with Twain's favorite theme of appearance and reality,
       and it can heighten interest, suspense, and realism in a dramatic scene. The

134

modern reader, equipped with a basic understanding of kinesics, experiences the richness and vitality of Twain's writing; he partakes in the 'total' communication of literature. (Eschholz 1973: 8)

This is a comment on Twain's genius for employing descriptive body language in his writings. Considering the influence Twain's work exerted on Hemingway's literary style, it may safely be assumed that what is true for Twain is to some extent true for Hemingway as well. Furthermore, a thorough examination of body language in Hemingway's works could be one effective way to more deeply understand his works since it enables us to take part in the total communication of his literature as Eschholz observed about Twain.

In this paper, after this introductory section, section 2 will discuss previous research on body language in literature. Then, section 3 will look at the general usage of body language in American literature, as roughly seen through the comparison of some American authors, including Hemingway, Twain, Willa Cather and F. Scott Fitzgerald. Specifically, submodes of body language, or facial expressions and eye behavior (Korte 1997: 37–8), will be examined using several electric corpora and a concordancer, with the main attention being given to the authors' short stories. Finally, section 4 will examine, as a case study, examples of facial expressions and eye behavior found in Hemingway's breakthrough novel, *The Sun Also Rises*, taking due account of the plot development and the context in which those examples appear.

1.1. Corpus and concordancer

All the self-made corpora in this paper, excepting those concerning Hemingway, were downloaded from Project Gutenberg (http://www. gutenberg.org/wiki/Main_Page) and Project Gutenberg Australia (http:// gutenberg.net.au./). These corpora were analyzed using the concordancer AntConc 3.2.4w (http://www.antlab.sci.waseda.ac.jp/software.html). The following are the e-texts contained in each corpus:

Hemingway's Novels Corpus (henceforth HNC, Total word tokens: 513,424)
The Torrents of Spring (1926), *The Sun Also Rises* (1926), *A Farewell to Arms*

(1929), *To Have and Have Not* (1937), *For Whom the Bell Tolls* (1940), *Across the River and into the Trees* (1950), *The Old Man and the Sea* (1952)

Hemingway's Short Stories Corpus (henceforth HSSC, Total word tokens: 146,915)
'The Short Happy Life of Francis Macomber,' 'The Capital of the World,' 'The Snows of Kilimanjaro,' 'Old Man at the Bridge,' 'Up in Michigan,' 'On the Quai at Smyrna,' 'Indian Camp,' 'The Doctor and the Doctor's Wife,' 'The End of Something,' 'The Three-Day Blow,' 'The Battler,' 'A Very Short Story,' 'Soldier's Home,' 'The Revolutionist,' 'Mr. and Mrs. Elliot,' 'Cat in the Rain,' 'Out of Season,' 'Cross-Country Snow,' 'My Old Man,' 'Big Two-Hearted River: Part I,' 'Big Two-Hearted River: Part II,' 'The Undefeated,' 'In Another Country,' 'Hills Like White Elephants,' 'The Killers,' 'Che Ti Dice La Patria?,' 'Fifty Grand,' 'A Simple Enquiry,' 'Ten Indians,' 'A Canary for One,' 'An Alpine Idyll,' 'A Pursuit Race,' 'Today is Friday,' 'Banal Story,' 'Now I Lay Me,' 'After the Storm,' 'A Clean, Well-Lighted Place,' 'The Light of the World,' 'God Rest You Merry, Gentlemen,' 'The Sea Change,' 'A Way You'll Never Be,' 'The Mother of a Queen,' 'One Reader Writes,' 'Homage to Switzerland,' 'A Day's Wait,' 'A Natural History of the Dead,' 'Wine of Wyoming,' 'The Gambler, the Nun, and the Radio,' 'Fathers and Sons'

Twain's Novels Corpus (henceforth TNC, Total word tokens: 592,706)
The Adventures of Tom Sawyer (1876), *Adventures of Huckleberry Finn* (1885), *A Connecticut Yankee in King Arthur's Court* (1889), *The Tragedy of Pudd'nhead Wilson* (1894), *Tom Sawyer Abroad* (1894), *Personal Recollections of Joan of Arc* (1895), *Tom Sawyer, Detective* (1896), *The Man That Corrupted Hadleyburg* (1900)

Twain's Short Stories Corpus (henceforth TSSC, Total word tokens: 170,660)
'A Burlesque Biography,' 'A Cure for the Blues,' 'A Curious Dream,' 'A Dog's Tale,' 'A Fable,' 'A Helpless Situation,' 'A Humane Word from Satan,' 'A Letter to the Secretary of the Treasury,' 'A Medieval Romance,' 'A Monument to Adam,' 'A Mysterious Visit,' 'A Telephonic Conversation,' 'A True Story,' 'Advice to Little Girls,' 'Amended Obituaries,' 'An Entertaining Article,' 'Cannibalism in the Cars,' 'Does the Race of Man Love a Lord?,' 'The Story of the Good Little Boy,' 'Edward Mills and George Benton: A Tale,' 'Eve's Diary,' 'Extracts from Adam's Diary,' 'General Washington's Negro Body-Servant,' 'How to Tell a Story,' 'Hunting the Deceitful Turkey,' 'Introduction to "The

New Guide of the Conversation in Portuguese and English",' 'Is He Living or Is He Dead?,' 'Journalism in Tennessee,' 'Italian with Grammar,' 'Italian without a Master,' 'Luck,' 'Niagara,' 'Political Economy,' 'Portrait of King William III,' 'Post-Mortem Poetry,' 'The $30,000 Bequest,' 'A Ghost Story,' 'Science Vs. Luck,' 'The Californian's Tale,' 'The Celebrated Jumping Frog,' 'The Danger of Lying in Bed,' 'The Enemy Conquered; or, Love Triumphant,' 'The Esquimau Maiden's Romance,' 'The Facts in the Case of the Great Beef Contract,' 'The First Writing-Machines,' 'The Five Boons of Life,' 'My Watch,' 'The Man That Corrupted Hadleyburg,' 'The Story of the Bad Little Boy,' 'The McWilliamses and the Burglar Alarm,' 'Travelling with a Reformer,' 'Was It Heaven? or Hell?,' 'Wit-Inspirations of the "Two-Year-Olds"'

Cather's Short Stories Corpus (henceforth CSSC, Total word tokens: 172,142)
'Peter,' 'On the Divide,' 'Eric Hermannson's Soul,' 'The Sentimentality of William Tavener,' 'The Namesake,' 'The Enchanted Bluff,' 'The Joy of Nelly Deane,' 'The Bohemian Girl,' 'Consequences,' 'The Bookkeeper's Wife,' 'Ardessa,' 'Her Boss,' 'Coming, Aphrodite!,' 'The Diamond Mine,' 'A Gold Slipper,' 'Scandal,' 'Paul's Case,' 'A Wagner Matinee,' 'The Sculptor's Funeral,' 'A Death in the Desert,' 'Flavia and Her Artists,' 'The Garden Lodge,' 'The Marriage of Phaedra'

Fitzgerald's Short Stories Corpus (henceforth FSSC, Total word tokens: 152,152)
'The Offshore Pirate,' 'The Ice Palace,' 'Head and Shoulders,' 'The Cut-Glass Bowl,' 'Bernice Bobs Her Hair,' 'Benediction,' 'Dalyrimple Goes Wrong,' 'The Four Fists,' 'The Jelly-Bean,' 'The Camel's Back,' 'May Day,' 'Porcelain and Pink,' 'The Diamond as Big as the Ritz,' 'The Curious Case of Benjamin Button,' 'Tarquin of Cheapside,' 'O Russet Witch!,' 'The Lees of Happiness,' 'Mr. Icky,' 'Jemina, the Mountain Girl'

The HNC is comprised of seven novels which were published when the author was alive, while the HSSC contains his forty-nine short stories from *The First Forty-Nine Stories* (1944). The TNC, compiled for my previous research (Takeshita 2016), includes Twain's eight novels, except for what is commonly known as *The Mysterious Stranger*, Twain's posthumous novel. *The Prince and the Pauper* (1881) was also excluded from the TNC according to the aim of the research. The TSSC is composed of Twain's fifty-three short stories, while the CSSC contains Cather's twenty-three short stories. The FSSC contains nineteen short stories from Fitzgerald's *Flappers and Philosophers* (1920) and *Tales of the Jazz Age* (1922). Cather and Fitzgerald may be regarded as Hemingway's contemporary writers.

2. Previous research
There are several studies of body language in English and American literature which have been conducted in some cases by taking advantage of a computer-assisted approach. They were conducted, however, with the goal of throwing partial light on the body language of a single work or of a limited number of its pages. There has been little empirical or overall research conducted on the body language used by an individual author, not to mention the body language of the times.

Gliserman (1996) discusses the way the human body makes its appearance in novels and the message it transmits. In the four chapters of his book, he examines separately the body in four novels from the 18th to 20th centuries, *Robinson Crusoe* (1719), *Jane Eyre* (1847), *To the Lighthouse* (1927), and *The Chaneysville Incident* (1981), though his psychoanalytic viewpoint makes his approach rather different from mine. Also, Hardy (2007) discusses the possibility of gaining an understanding of the themes of Flannery O'Connor's works through computer-assisted analysis of the author's use of grammatical voice and body language. Korte (1997) deals with many examples of body language mainly from English drama and novels, with minute attention paid to the context as well as the background of the period. Her analytical comments on excerpts, though not exactly statistically supported, are very suggestive, reminding us of the importance of engaging in a close reading of the texts. Moreover, Culpeper (2001), in a chapter under the title of 'Textual Cues in Characterization,' pays attention to 'visual features' used by Shakespeare, and discusses their key role for person perception (i.e., the way we form impressions of others) and characterization. Recently, Mahlberg (2013) has made an analysis of the language of Charles Dickens on the basis of corpus stylistics. In a chapter titled 'Body

Language,' she describes the framework of body language shown by Korte (1997) and discusses the role of body language in characterization. Moreover, by analyzing 'Body Part clusters' containing body-part nouns, she argues the importance of body language that is not easy to notice by the reader and accordingly has not gained much attention in the literature, as well as the importance of idiosyncratic body language.

The previous research mentioned above provides a foundation for my research; however, an attempt to accurately capture literary changes in the use of body language across time and authors, and to identify the development of body language as a form of literary expression, has only just started with our project.

3. Words for facial expressions and eye behavior found in corpora

Body-part nouns such as *hand(s)*, *head*, *eyes*, and *face* are generally found among the 100 highest-frequency content words in every literary work, though of course ranking is contingent on the authors, the works themselves and the times. Verbs like *looked* and *saw*, essential for describing the eye behavior of characters, are also found in the top 100 on the whole.[1]

In Hori (2004: 34–6), for example, among the 100 highest-frequency content words of Dickens, five word types for body parts such as *hand* (ranked 26), *head* (29), *face* (37), *eyes* (43), and *hands* (84) are found, with four out of the five ranking in the top 50. On the other hand, as for Twain, these word types are never ranked in the top 50 of the TNC: *head* (ranked 54), *hand* (72), *face* (76), and *hands* (92). *Eyes* is not found even in the top 100. What is more interesting about his novels is that *The Prince and the Pauper*, his 'most intricately plotted book' (Fisher 1983: xv), uses rather different facial expressions from his other novels. *Face* and *eyes* are ranked in much higher positions at 22nd and 24th, respectively, indicating that we should be aware of them as essential elements in creating the distinctively tense atmosphere of the text (Takeshita 2016).

---

[1] Needless to say, the semantic domain of each word is not obvious without any consideration of context. Such a detailed semantic analysis, however, goes beyond the scope of this paper. My present aim is, except for some contextual examinations made in section 4, to give an overview of words in the corpora.

As I touched on above, verbs of visual perception like *looked* and *saw* are frequently used to portray characters' eye behavior. For example, among the 100 highest-frequency content words, *looked* and *saw* are ranked 47th and 94th in The Dickens Corpus (Hori 2004), and 89th and 88th in the TNC (Takeshita 2016), though sometimes their frequency varies in a significant way.

Incidentally, when analysis of body language in literature is done, a collocational approach seems to be one of the most effective ways (see Hori 2004 and Mahlberg 2013). For instance, in English and American literature, as one conventional way to depict a character's state of mind, examples of *eyes* have been frequently combined with verbs such as 'flash,' 'blaze,' 'sparkle,' 'twinkle,' 'burn,' and so on, with these collocates often taking the *-ing* form as a participial adjective. Indeed, these combinations may be common and rather banal, even if present in literature, but how they are employed depends on the author. Twain's *The Prince and the Pauper* is a good example in which the common but contextually significant collocation of *eyes* and 'flash' lends itself to reflecting the personalities of and the subtle changes of mind of the two main characters in the story (Takeshita 2016).

On the other hand, among the 438 examples of *eyes* in Hemingway's works,[2] only seven are of such collocates; rather unvariedly, five out of the seven take 'shine' and the others 'brighten' and 'glisten.' What is more, these seven collocates are all verbs and consequently never modify *eyes* as a participial adjective ending in *-ing*. However, Fitzgerald, though also being a 'lost generation' author along with Hemingway, utilizes such a conventional collocation much more frequently and variedly.

We may assume from this fact that Hemingway tries as much as possible not to use common collocations of *eyes* as a means of disclosing characters' inner states. The reason for this is not hard to see; it is unrealistic to think that our physical eyes give off brilliance, thus betraying our states of mind.

Here it may be worth pointing out, in passing, the following fact. The

---

[2] Hereafter, when mention is made of Hemingway's 'works,' they indicate, to be exact, his 70 short stories, including *The First Forty-Nine Stories*, and his seven novels in the HNC published while alive.

Corpus of Historical American English (COHA) (http://corpus.byu. edu/coha/) shows that the frequency of the combination 'flashing eyes' or 'eyes flashing' is clearly low starting around 1920, as compared to its use in the 19th century. If this observation is correct, and a conventional way of depicting a character's state of mind has been truly decreasing in frequency over time, it is an intriguing fact from the perspective of the change and development of body language in literature. However, further research and minute analysis about this case is needed.

3.1. Comparative analysis of word frequencies using the corpora of short stories

When we try to grasp an author's literary style comprehensively, it is essential that the author's short stories also be discussed in detail. Twain, for example, has written many short stories as included in the TSSC, while Hemingway has often been mentioned as an expert short-story writer. Certainly, even though they are written by the same author, the linguistic and stylistic features of their short stories may not always be analogous to the quality of their novels, probably on account of the limited length of short stories. In this section, however, we will attempt to shed comparative light on several authors' short stories using some corpora in order to gain a comprehensive understanding of Hemingway's style as a whole, and hopefully take some cues for the following case study of Hemingway's facial expressions and eye behavior used in his novel, *The Sun Also Rises*.

Table 1, which is a translated, slightly modified reprint of that presented by Takeshita (2015), displays the result of comparing the HSSC with the TSSC, the CSSC, and the FSSC using AntConc. As one of its functions, AntConc extracts words, showing their automatically calculated keyness, which identifies keywords or negative keywords which appear statistically significantly more frequently or infrequently in the HSSC than in the TSSC, the CSSC, and the FSSC. Paying attention to these words, therefore, can help us obtain useful clues for the literary interpretation of Hemingway's short stories. The author's keywords and negative keywords indicative of body parts are shown below in decreasing order of keyness.

Table 1. Keywords and negative keywords indicative of body parts in the HSSC

Comparison with TSSC		Comparison with CSSC		Comparison with FSSC	
Keyword	*Negative keyword*	*Keyword*	*Negative keyword*	*Keyword*	*Negative keyword*
back	cheek	back	**eyes**	back	**eyes**
nose		leg	chin	leg	hair
head		legs	hair	belly	cheeks
chest		belly	cheeks	legs	feet
belly		nose	shoulders	head	arms
legs		mouth	teeth	nose	lips
shoulders		thighs	elbow	breasts	faces
face			brows	thigh	chin
shoulder			forehead	thighs	lip
beard			knee	chest	fists
toes					teeth
neck					
knees					
fingers					
hand					
hands					

As Table 1 shows, there is a clear difference in the comparative results between Twain, Cather, and Fitzgerald. Hemingway's *eyes* is not listed as a negative keyword in comparison with the TSSC and yet at the same time it is ranked first when compared with the CSSC and the FSSC. Concerning Twain, this result may indicate that his use of body-part nouns for facial expressions are low in frequency. Furthermore, Table 1 allows us to discover the interesting fact that quite a few body-part nouns for facial expressions such as *chin*, *cheeks*, *lip(s)*, *teeth*, *brows*, *forehead*, *faces*, and *hair* are listed as Hemingway's negative keywords compared with the CSSC and the FSSC. It may be said that concerning the use of body-part nouns for facial expressions, the word *eyes*, in particular, which should be an essential non-verbal device for effectively describing a character's state of mind, is used rather sparingly in Hemingway's short stories.

142

Now, we will throw additional light on the author's use of the word *eyes* in the HSSC so as to find something characteristic other than its relative low frequency. Interestingly enough, as mentioned before, Hemingway seldom combines the word *eyes* with verbs expressing degrees of brightness in his works. Especially, in spite of their conventional use, we never find examples of *eyes* modified by participial adjectives ending in *-ing*, which stem from such verbs. Therefore, examples of the collocation of *eye(s)* and an adjectival modifier just before it will be thoroughly dealt with here to lay a foundation for my further research. On this occasion, we will also look at instances of *face*, as representative of body-part nouns for facial expressions.

Table 2 presents the frequency of *eye(s)* and *face* per 100,000 words and the percentage modified by an adjective next to them on the left in each corpus.[3]

Table 2. Frequency of *eye(s)* and *face* per 100,000 words and the percentage of them modified by an adjective next to them on the left

	Freq. of eyes	Adj. + eyes	Freq. of eye	Adj. + eye	Freq. of face	Adj. + face
HSSC	64.6	0.13% (13/95)	17.6	0.23% (6/26)	94.6	0.18% (26/139)
TSSC	50.3	0.29% (25/86)	32.2	0.29% (16/55)	56.8	0.16% (16/97)
CSSC	117.9	0.35% (73/203)	16.2	0.42% (12/28)	108.0	0.31% (58/186)
FSSC	170.2	0.32% (83/259)	16.4	0.32% (8/25)	78.2	0.26% (31/119)

Table 2 reveals a much lower frequency in Hemingway's use of *eyes* (64.6), compared with the CSSC (117.9) and the FSSC (170.2), mirroring the result in Table 1, where *eyes* tops the list of body-part nouns as a negative keyword. Concerning *face*, Hemingway (94.6) is not so largely different in frequency from Cather (108.0) and Fitzgerald (78.2). When

---

[3] Words which can be grouped into a determiner, including *all*, *every*, *other*, *own*, and so on, are excluded here.

143

the discussion is confined to frequency, Twain's *eyes* (50.3) and *face* (56.8) are lower than Hemingway's. However, what should be noticed here is that the percentages of body-part nouns modified by an adjective just before them are consistently low in the HSSC, especially making a clear distinction from those in the CSSC and the FSSC. It is not so difficult for us to theorize that the main cause of this result stems from Hemingway's 'hard-boiled' style. In the following section, examples from each corpus are described for reference:[4]

Examples in the HSSC
EYES : amused eyes, batting eyes, blood-shot eyes, blue eyes (2), bright eyes, cold eyes, fine eyes, flat eyes, pig eyes, wicked eyes, wonderful eyes, yellow eyes
EYE: black eye (4), human eye, right eye
FACE: American face, bloody face (2), brown face (2), dusty face, fine face, good-looking face, heavy face, last face, lined face, mutilated face, oiled face, open face, oval face, pale face (2), potato face, prettiest face, pretty face, red face (3), well-loved face, white face (2)

Examples in the TSSC
EYES: accusing eyes, admiring eyes (2), affectionate eyes, bleary eyes, blue eyes (2), brilliant eyes, closed eyes, dry eyes, earnest eyes, fascinated eyes, happy eyes (2), honest eyes, lovely eyes, lowered eyes, lying eyes, old eyes, sad eyes, startled eyes, suspicious eyes, tired eyes, vacant eyes, wondering eyes
EYE: eagle eye, flashing eye, Glass eye, Hog-Eye, hungry eye, intelligent eye (2), penetrating eye (2), public eye, reproving eye, sharp eye, steady eye, suspicious eye, tired eye, watchful eye
FACE: black face, contented face, dead face (2), drawn face, girlish face, good face, innocent face, leonine face, long face, lovely face, picture face, sad face, sweet face (2), trim-chiseled face

Examples in the CSSC
EYES: abominable eyes, alert eyes, almond eyes (3), black eyes (6), blood-shot eyes, blue eyes (4), bright eyes (2), brilliant eyes, brown eyes, burning eyes, cherishing eyes, clear eyes, confident eyes, curious eyes, dark eyes, deep-set

---

[4] Numbers in brackets indicate number of occurrences.

eyes, dim eyes, downcast eyes, dull eyes (3), fishy eyes, flashing eyes (2), gray eyes (4), green eyes, half-closed eyes (3), hazel eyes (2), impatient eyes, keen eyes, kind eyes, little eyes (3), mysterious eyes, near-sighted eyes, pale eyes, pale-blue eyes (3), remarkable eyes, restless eyes, round eyes (3), searching eyes, slanting eyes, sleepy eyes (2), Spanish eyes, twinkling eyes, uncomprehending eyes, wandering eyes, watery eyes, yellow eyes, yellow-brown eyes

EYE: appraising eye (2), blood-shot eye, blue eye, bright eye, clear eye, discerning eye, lighting eye, liquid eye, outward eye, public eye, sharp eye

FACE: apoplectic face, bearded face, bestial face, blue-veined face, bold-featured face, boyish face, bronzed face, brown face, 'business' face, clean-cut face, clean-shaven face, close-sealed face, disconsolate face, distressed face, emaciated face, florid face, flushed face (3), gentle face, golden face, grey face, haggard face, half-averted face, handsome face, historic face, hypocritical face, intelligent face, little face (2), long face (2), lupine face, mournful face, old face, pale face, pressed-brick-and-cement face, pretty face, quivering face, red face, riding-dress face, rock face, round face, rugged face, sensitive face, square face, Sugar face, tense face, thin face, tired face, unusual face, vigorous face, well-bred face, well-known face, white face, worse face, wry face, youthful face

Examples in the FSSC

EYES: active eyes, averted eyes, baby eyes, beautiful eyes, blazing eyes, blind eyes, blood-shot eyes, blue eyes (8), brown eyes (5), china eyes, curious eyes, dark eyes (7), dazed eyes, deep-set eyes, distraught eyes, dull eyes, exquisite eyes, faded eyes, far-away eyes (2), fearsome eyes, frigid eyes, gray eyes (12), hollow eyes, horror-stricken eyes, intelligent eyes (2), intent eyes, joyless eyes, murderous eyes, old eyes, owlish eyes, piercing eyes (2), pure eyes, rat-eyes, reproachful eyes, shadowy eyes (3), sharp eyes, single eyes, sparkling eyes, startled eyes, stony eyes, sympathetic eyes, tawny eyes (3), twinkling eyes, uncertain eyes, watery eyes (2), welcoming eyes, wide-open eyes

EYE: blue eye, glass eye, glazed eye, green eye, malignant eye, public eye, quizzical eye, steady eye

FACE: appetizing face, cardboard face, cheerful face, chinless face, cobwebbed face, dark face, elfish face, fair face, fairylike face, flowery face, handsome face, huge face, icy-cold face, intent face, little face, meanest face, medicinal face, pale face, pallid face, scarred face, sensitive face, set face, tabby-cat face, tear-stained face, tear-wet face, vacuous face (2), white face, whole face, young face (2)

When we look at examples in the HSSC, adjectives expressive of appearance and color seem to be conspicuous, while there are few expressing states of mind or mentality, such as *amused* and *wicked*. Although, in the case of Twain, the frequency of his *eyes* and *face* is lower than that of Hemingway's, as far as examples of *eyes* go, we can easily find various different kinds of adjectives from those in the HSSC, including *accusing, admiring, affectionate, suspicious*, and others. When it comes to examples in the CSSC and the FSSC, a variety of adjectives, which indicate appearance and inner states of mind, are there, together with participial adjectives of brilliance such as *blazing, flashing, sparkling, twinkling*, and so on.

Now our attention will be turned to verbs of visual perception, a significant contributor to the expressions of eye behavior in literature. Table 3 lists the verbs in the HSSC extracted as keywords and negative keywords.[5]

Table 3. Verbs of visual perception in the HSSC extracted as keywords and negative keywords

Comparison with TSSC		Comparison with CSSC		Comparison with FSSC	
Keyword					
Word type	*Keyness*	*Word type*	*Keyness*	*Word type*	*Keyness*
looked	239.942	looked	43.086	looked	107.714
looking	90.715	looking	19.949	looking	33.953
watched	51.890	watched	8.519	watched	20.154
saw	18.245	see	7.238	saw	10.813
watching	18.119	watching	6.572	watching	8.266
				seen	8.101

---

[5] Table 3 is a translated reprint from Takeshita (2015) with a slight change in layout.

Table 3. Continued

Comparison with TSSC		Comparison with CSSC		Comparison with FSSC	
Negative keyword					
Word type	Keyness	Word type	Keyness	Word type	Keyness
gazed	11.583	glanced	17.548	stared	20.667
glanced	10.399	staring	11.030	glanced	9.709
looks	7.443			gazed	8.235

Verbs expressing visual perception in the HSSC—'watch,' 'look,' and 'see'—are different in terms of keyness and word type, and appear with high frequency when compared with each corpus. This result seems to represent an important facet of Hemingway's body language in his short stories. Put plainly, in his short stories, *eyes*, a word essential for facial expressions, is relatively low in frequency, whereas basic verbs of visual perception vital for describing eye behavior occur with high frequency. Of course, the same is not always true of body language in every literary text. Gliserman (1996: 12–13), for example, points out that *Jane Eyre* has a high frequency of the body-part noun *eyes*, as well as a high frequency of 'verbs associated with seeing and looking,' resulting in their salient redundancy. Finally, another aspect not to lose sight of here is that Hemingway has a clearly selective leaning toward basic verbs of visual perception such as 'watch,' 'look,' and 'see' instead of verbs such as 'gaze,' 'glance,' and 'stare,' which are extracted as negative keywords in Table 3.

4. A case study of *The Sun Also Rises*

This section will focus its attention, as a case study, on one of Hemingway's novels, *The Sun Also Rises*, which was published during the same period as that of his major short stories in the HSSC, and won him distinction as a novelist. Young Americans living in Paris, their wasteful and unfruitful activities in the dating world, and their visit to bullfights in Spain are described. In this novel, can we once again identify several features of the author's body language discussed previously? Are there

147

any stylistic devices beyond them to impress on us the personality of the characters and their inner states of mind? These questions will be examined with special attention to the context and the plot of the story.

4.1. The 100 highest-frequency content words in *The Sun Also Rises*

First of all, content words making the top 100 in frequency in *The Sun Also Rises* are presented for consideration in Table 4.[6]

Table 4. The 100 highest-frequency content words in *The Sun Also Rises*

Rank	Word type	Tokens	Rank	Word type	Tokens	Rank	Word type	Tokens
1	said	966	36	night	91	69	stairs	64
2	went	298	37	way	90	72	morning	63
3	bull	244	38	drink	89	73	old	62
4	go	237	39	hell	86	73	really	62
5	good	232	40	took	85	73	stood	62
6	know	212	41	tell	84	76	take	61
7	get	204	42	**saw**	83	77	**hand**	58
8	no	201	42	started	83	77	stopped	58
9	then	193	44	wanted	82	79	bed	57
10	going	192	45	again	80	80	day	56
11	back	190	45	crowd	80	80	money	56
12	came	188	45	long	80	80	side	56
13	very	172	48	hotel	79	83	bottle	55
14	come	170	48	**look**	79	83	first	55
15	**see**	164	50	away	78	83	trees	55
16	got	161	51	town	77	86	ever	54
17	just	155	52	**looking**	76	86	feel	54
18	asked	147	52	sat	76	86	white	54
19	**looked**	138	54	big	75	89	car	53

---

[6] Content words are based on ones which could be classified into *open classes* and *numerals* by Quirk et al. (1985: 67). Proper nouns and words for which it is difficult to identify part of speech, including *have, so, do, be, all, one*, and *there*, are excluded. Owing to the existence of the contracted form *n't, not* is also excluded.

148

Table 4. Continued

Rank	Word type	Tokens	Rank	Word type	Tokens	Rank	Word type	Tokens
20	right	130	55	man	74	90	dark	52
21	time	126	55	walked	74	90	fine	52
22	people	125	57	turned	73	92	ring	51
23	want	122	58	bulls	70	93	drunk	50
24	say	121	59	always	68	93	fight	50
25	think	116	59	made	68	93	read	50
26	yes	115	61	count	67	96	felt	49
27	let	113	61	door	67	96	left	49
28	two	112	61	make	67	96	thing	49
29	too	108	64	three	66	96	thought	49
30	put	107	65	**face**	65	100	damned	48
31	never	105	65	**head**	65	100	give	48
32	room	96	65	road	65	100	sitting	48
32	street	96	65	square	65	100	talk	48
34	table	95	69	café	64			
34	wine	95	69	nice	64			

As Table 4 clearly shows, body-part nouns are not ranked in the top 50 at all; *face* and *head* are tied at 65th and *hand* is 77th. *Eyes* is not even found in the top 100. Several word forms of 'look' and 'see,' such as *looked* (ranked 19), *saw* (42), and *look* (48), can be found in the top 50, except for *looking* (52). This enables us to recognize an almost similar inclination of Hemingway's wording in his short stories, where a comparatively low frequency of *eyes* and a high frequency of basic verbs of visual perception can be observed in general.

4.2. Collocations of *eye(s)*

First, we will closely observe how examples of the term *eye(s)*, which is not listed in Table 4 in spite of its intrinsic high potential as a facial expression, are actually employed in *The Sun Also Rises*. In fact, Hemingway uses *eyes* 35 times and *eye* seven times in the novel. The following adjective is one which collocates with *eyes* just before it:

149

The Sun Also Rises (Total word tokens: 70,358):
EYES (1/35, 0.02): contemptuous eyes
EYE (0/7, 0): none

Among the 35 examples of *eyes*, only one has an adjectival modifier just before it, the percentage of the occurrence being 2%, while the seven examples of *eye* do not contain any adjectives in that position. We will throw contextual light on this example of an adjective of mentality, *contemptuous*, in detail later. In any case, this restraint in using adjectives reminds us again of the author's strict 'hard-boiled' style, as already shown in Table 2. For reference, given in chronological order are examples of 'adjective + *eye(s)*,' found in Hemingway's other novels, *The Torrents of Spring* (1926), *A Farewell to Arms* (1929), *To Have and Have Not* (1937), *For Whom the Bell Tolls* (1940), *Across the River and into the Trees* (1950) and *The Old Man and the Sea* (1952), all of which were published while he was still alive:

The Torrents of Spring (Total word tokens: 21,905):
EYES (1/23, 0.04): keen eyes
EYE (1/1, 1): yellow eye

A Farewell to Arms (Total word tokens: 91,374):
EYES (3/27, 0.11): black eyes, gray eyes, shut eyes
EYE (1/1, 1): right eye

To Have and Have Not (Total word tokens: 57,564):
EYES (5/19, 0.26): blue eyes, gray eyes, narrow eyes (2), tear-reddened eyes
EYE (0/4, 0): none

For Whom the Bell Tolls (Total word tokens: 175,941):
EYES (43/136, 0.31): bleary eyes, blue eyes (7), cat-eyes, closed eyes (2), close-set eyes, dark eyes (2), droopy eyes, gray eyes (6), hawk eyes, little eyes, merry eyes, odd eyes, pig-eyes (5), proud eyes, quiet eyes, red-rimmed eyes, sad eyes, set eyes, small eyes, staring eyes, sunken eyes, unblinking eyes, watery eyes, yellow eyes, yellow-brown eyes, yellow-gray eyes
EYE (2/9, 0.22): left eye, puffed eye

150

Across the River and into the Trees (Total word tokens: 69,417):

EYES (14/28, 0.5): blue eyes, hooded eyes, hopeless eyes, hostile eyes, Italian eyes, journalistic eyes, metallic eyes, old eyes, protruding eyes, steel eyes, strange eyes (2), stupid eyes, truthful eyes

EYE (6/10, 0.6): glass eye (3), huge eye, left eye, lost eye

The Old Man and the Sea (Total word tokens: 26,865):

EYES (6/24, 0.25): cat-like eyes, loving eyes, pig eyes, strange eyes, unintelligent eyes, yellow eyes

EYE (1/10, 0.1): left eye

The frequency of *eyes* per 10,000 words in each novel varies as follows: *The Torrents of Spring* 10.4, *The Sun Also Rises* 4.9, *A Farewell to Arms* 2.9, *To Have and Have Not* 3.3, *For Whom the Bell Tolls* 7.7, *Across the River and into the Trees* 4.0, and *The Old Man and the Sea* 8.9. However, the point to observe here is that the percentages of the collocation 'adjective + *eyes*' are similarly low in *The Torrents of Spring* (0.04), *The Sun Also Rises* (0.02), and *A Farewell to Arms* (0.11). They were published in the 1920s, almost the same period as the author's main short stories in the HSSC (0.13).[7]

With this in mind, we will now examine how the author uses the body-part noun in each context. At the beginning, our attention will be paid again to the adjective of mentality *contemptuous* collocating with *eyes*:

(2) [. . .] he had saluted the President with the same wolf-jawed smile and ***contemptuous eyes***, and handed his sword over the barrera to be wiped, [. . .][8] (Ch. 18)

This quotation (2) comes from the context where the facial expressions of a matador, Belmonte, are minutely described. He is unpopular and much disliked among spectators compared with Romero, a young and very popular matador. Hemingway uses the adjective *contemptuous* only eight

---

[7] See Table 2.

[8] Hereafter, bold-faced italics in all quotations are mine.

151

times in his works, and its collocation with *eyes* never occurs except in the case of this quotation. The following is a long but useful quotation, including (2), which may help us better recognize the author's delicate way of introducing such a rare collocation:

(3) Also Belmonte imposed conditions and insisted that his bulls should not be too large, nor too dangerously armed with horns, and so the element that was necessary to give the sensation of tragedy was not there, and the public, who wanted three times as much from Belmonte, who was sick with a fistula, as Belmonte had ever been able to give, felt defrauded and cheated, and Belmonte's jaw came further out in *contempt*, and his face turned yellower, and he moved with greater difficulty as his pain increased, and finally the crowd were actively against him, and he was utterly *contemptuous* and indifferent. [. . .] Sometimes he turned to smile that toothed, long-jawed, lipless smile when he was called something particularly insulting, and always the pain that any movement produced grew stronger and stronger, until finally his yellow face was parchment color, and after his second bull was dead and the throwing of bread and cushions was over, after he had saluted the President with the same wolf-jawed smile and *contemptuous eyes*, and handed his sword over the barrera to be wiped, and put back in its case, he passed through into the callejon and leaned on the barrera below us, [. . .] (Ch. 18)

The public's harsh and stinging response to Belmonte's bullfight and his strong reaction to them are described in detail. The collocation *contemptuous eyes* is used to express Belmonte's repulsive behavior. Here, if we widen our view and make a detailed observation of the context as a whole, we find that the noun *contempt* and the adjective *contemptuous* are employed previously to portray Belmonte. Interestingly enough, Hemingway seems to make a stylistically regardful arrangement for the introduction of his very rare collocation *contemptuous eyes* by means of utilizing the noun *contempt* and the adjective *contemptuous* in advance.

Next comes a different type of example of *eyes* from the one above, whose collocational scope, without being confined to the adjective just before *eyes*, is broadened for the further potential devices of the author. The following quotations may serve as good examples:

152

(4) Brett looked at me and **wrinkled up the corners of her eyes**. (Ch. 7)

(5) '[. . .],' Brett smiled at him, **wrinkling the corners of her eyes**. (Ch. 8)

(6) Brett **wrinkled up the corners of her eyes** at him. (Ch. 8)

(7) Brett gestured at him [. . .] and **wrinkled the corners of her eyes**. (Ch. 8)

(8) Brett looking at him quite coolly, but **the corners of her eyes** were smiling. (Ch. 8)

All the instances in *The Sun Also Rises* which contain the noun phrase *the corners of her eyes* are exemplified in (4)–(8). Except for (8), the noun phrase occurs with the verb (phrase) 'wrinkle (up)' as its grammatical object. In addition, in all of the quotations above, the personal pronoun *her* of *her eyes* indicates one of the main characters, Brett, who magically fascinates men around her in the story. Other than these five instances, we have only three similar collocations in Hemingway's works: *the corners of his eyes* in *To Have and Have Not*, and *the corners of his eyes* and *the corners of each eye* in *Across the River and into the Trees*.[9] They are all employed, however, for men's facial expressions, and never serve as a grammatical object of 'wrinkle (up).'

Another interesting example is given below, in which the verb 'crinkle,'[10] a synonym for the verb 'wrinkle,' co-occurs with, again, Brett's *eyes*:

(9) Brett saw us coming and waved. **Her eyes crinkled up** as we came to the table. (Ch. 13)

Except for this single instance, Hemingway never uses the verb 'crinkle' in his works. In examples (4)–(9), which are put in order of appearance in the novel, *the corners of her eyes* in (4)–(7) functions, at first, as a grammatical object of the transitive verb 'wrinkle (up),' and then, in (8), it changes its role to a grammatical subject. At last, in (9), *her eyes* without *the corners of* works alone as a grammatical subject as if in fact her eyes

---

[9] One more instance of *the corners of his eyes* in 'One Trip Across' is not mentioned here in order to avoid double counting, as the short story was published again later as part one in *To Have and Have Not*.

[10] *OED2* s.v. Crinkle I.1.

153

are working automatically and independently from their owner, Brett. Hemingway's intensive use of almost the same or analogous expressions for Brett seems to do much for creating her distinctive mood and the magical attraction essential for her character development in *The Sun Also Rises*.

4.3. Collocations of *face*

This section devotes itself to an investigation into examples of another important body-part noun, *face*. First, all the examples of the collocation 'adjective + *face*' found in the HNC are given below:

The Torrents of Spring:
FACE (4/17, 0.23): black face, dark face, grim face, lean face

The Sun Also Rises:
FACE (8/65, 0.12): awful face, drawn face, honest face, hurt face, Jewish face, pockmarked face, sullen face, yellow face

A Farewell to Arms:
FACE (9/63, 0.14): brown face (2), dark face, healthy-looking face, kind face, lovely face, nice face, thin face, whole face

To Have and Have Not:
FACE (15/59, 0.25): angry face, beautiful face (2), big face, freckled face, goddamn face (2), goddamned face, high-cheek-boned face, Irish face, pretty face, red face, reddish face, ruddy face, straight-nosed face

For Whom the Bell Tolls:
FACE (53/211, 0.25): beard-stubbled face, beautiful face (2), bending face, big face (3), bristly face (2), brown face (10), dark face, fat face, fear-drained face, flat face (3), Flemish face, good face, gray face (3), great face (3), gypsy face, hard face, hawk-nosed face, heavy face, left face, love-lazy face, lovely face, red face (2), round face, sad face, sagging face, smooth-lovely face, sun-burned face, thin face, ugly face, unshaved face, white face, wind-darkened face, wonderful face

154

Across the River and into the Trees:
> FACE (25/46, 0.54): breakheart face, caricature face, ebony face, emaciated face, Fascist face, fine face, gay face, grey face, happy face, inspiring face, lovely face, loving face, moon face, nicer face, pleasant face, ravaged face, strange face (2), transformable face, ugly face (3), un-choleric face, white face, wonderful face

The Old Man and the Sea:
> FACE (0/11, 0): none

The percentages of *face* collocating with an adjective next to it on the left in *The Sun Also Rises* (0.12) and in *A Farewell to Arms* (0.14) are, it seems, similarly low to the percentage in the HSSC (0.18).[11] This narrow scope of collocation easily makes known the author's restrained use of adjectives as a collocate of *face,* especially in *The Sun Also Rises*, as in the case of *eyes* observed in the previous section.

Accordingly, the collocational scope of *face* will be expanded here again so that we may see any resulting findings. Among 65 examples of *face* in *The Sun Also Rises*, 13 are those in which *face* as a node is semantically modified by color terms, as in (10)–(22):

(10) **Brett's face** was **white** and the long line of her neck showed in [. . .] (Ch. 4)

(11) [Cohn] stood up from the table **his face white**, and stood there white and angry [. . .] (Ch. 5)

(12) Cohn looked up as I went in. **His face** was **white**. (Ch. 6)

(13) Bill went off with Cohn. **Cohn's face** was **sallow**. (Ch. 13)

(14) [Cohn] was reserved and formal, and **his face** was still taut and **sallow**, [. . .] (Ch. 13)

(15) They both stood up. **Romero's face** was very **brown**. (Ch. 16)

(16) **[Cohn's]** **face** had the **sallow, yellow** look it got when he was insulted, [. . .] (Ch. 16)

(17) [Cohn] stood waiting, **his face sallow**, his hands fairly low, [. . .] (Ch. 16)

(18) **Bill's face** was **red**. 'Come back in, Edna,' he said. (Ch. 17)

(19) **[Cohn's]** **face** was **sallow** under the light. He was standing up. (Ch. 17)

---

[11] See Table 2.

(20) Belmonte looked ahead, **his face wan** and **yellow**, his long wolf jaw out. (Ch. 18)

(21) [. . .] Belmonte's jaw came further out in contempt, and **his face** turned **yellower**, [. . .] (Ch. 18)

(22) [. . .] finally **[Belmonte's]** **yellow face** was **parchment** color [. . .] (Ch. 18)

Seven out of the 13 examples of collocation in (11), (12), (13), (14), (16), (17) and (19) are intensively employed to depict the facial expressions of a Jewish man, Robert Cohn. The three instances in (20), (21) and (22) are used for Belmonte's facial expressions. The rest in (10), (15) and (18) are used for Brett, Romero, and Bill, respectively. Taking notice of the co-occurrence of *face* with a color term with wide collocational span elucidates the fact that such a way of using color terms for describing facial expressions is almost limited to the facial expressions of two idiosyncratic characters, namely Cohn, a disliked young American Jew, and Belmonte, an unpopular matador.

Regarding Belmonte, the recurrent collocations of his *face* and *yellow(er)*, with the help of other color terms like *wan* and *parchment*, serve to impress on us his bizarre appearance. More interestingly, concerning Cohn, his face color is described with the term *white* as in (11) and (12) in the early stages of the story, when he is angry or feels insulted. However, as the story progresses, when he becomes much disliked and disfavored by his acquaintances on account of his egocentric standpoint, his *face* begins to consistently collocate with the color term *sallow* as in (13), (14), (16), (17), and (19), though in (16) *yellow* co-occurs also. The word *sallow* is defined in *OED2* as '[h]aving a sickly yellow or brownish yellow colour.'[12] Cohn is almost at the end of his rope due to insults and provocations from his acquaintances, which in turn is responsible for his decisively adverse relationship with them. Hemingway's selectively predominant use of *sallow* as a collocate of Cohn's *face* in *The Sun Also Rises* makes a significant contribution to imprinting on us his troubled mind in such a situation. In fact, the author uses the color term *sallow* only 6 times in his works. Except for once in *For Whom the Bell Tolls*,

---

[12] *OED2* s.v. Sallow a.

156

where it collocates with *skin*, not *face*, the other times it is used are all in *The Sun Also Rises* merely for Cohn's facial expressions. Such a telling manner of presenting Cohn, not by revealing his mind easily with adjectives or adverbs of mentality, but through conveying it suggestively with the repetitive use of a color term for his face, enables us to feel more deeply and realistically Cohn's unintelligible mind and the emotional distance between him and his acquaintances.

4.4. Verbs of visual perception for eye behavior
This section will turn its attention to examples of verbs of visual perception. Hemingway's highly frequent and selective use of this type of verb in his short stories has been already mentioned before. Therefore, we will first examine here whether such a tendency can also be seen in the HNC. As a reference corpus (Total word tokens: 444,556), we will use one which is comprised of four novels: *My Ántonia* (1918) by Cather (1873–1947), *Main Street* (1920) by Sinclair Lewis (1885–1951), *Three Soldiers* (1921) by John Dos Passos (1896–1970), and *The Great Gatsby* (1925) by Fitzgerald (1896–1940). These authors may all be regarded as contemporaries of Hemingway (1899–1961), and each novel can be considered one of their representative works.

Table 5. Verbs of visual perception extracted as keywords and negative keywords in the HNC in comparison with a reference corpus, and their frequency per 100,000 words in each corpus

	Keyword and its frequency (per 100,000 words)			
Rank	*Word type*	*Keyness*	*Freq. in HNC*	*Freq. in ref. corpus*
1	looked	95.835	196.1	116.9
2	watched	77.908	43.4	13.4
3	see	55.010	228.8	161.7
4	saw	45.066	129.5	84.5
5	watching	22.037	26.4	13.0
6	looking	13.529	84.9	64.3
7	sighted	10.547	2.5	0.2

Table 5. Continued

Negative keyword and its frequency (per 100, 000 words)

Rank	Word type	Keyness	Freq. in HNC	Freq. in ref. corpus
1	glanced	76.983	0.9	15.7
2	stared	60.597	2.1	16.4
3	staring	57.531	1.7	14.8
4	glared	15.397	0.1	3.1
5	peeped	14.004	0.1	2.9
6	glancing	12.938	0.5	3.8
7	stare	9.438	0.3	2.6

All word types extracted as keywords in Table 5, except *sighted*, are basic verbs of visual perception, which can also be found as keywords in Table 3. Moreover, different verbs of visual perception other than these basic ones, such as 'glance,' 'stare,' 'glare,' and 'peep,' have all been extracted as negative keywords. This contrastive result clearly shows that Hemingway's selective use of basic verbs of visual perception for his characters' eye behavior is consistently made not only in his short stories but also in his novels.

Also, a cursory glance at these extracted negative keywords allows us to realize that they imply the characters' manner of looking, in contrast to basic verbs like 'look,' 'watch,' and 'see.' For example, 'glance'[13] means 'to cast a momentary look,' as defined in the *OED2*. Similarly, 'stare'[14] is defined as 'to gaze fixedly and with eyes wide open,' 'glare'[15] as '[t]o look fixedly and fiercely,' and 'peep'[16] as 'to look furtively, slyly, or pryingly.'

Taking into consideration that the author has a strong preference for basic verbs of perception, does this mean he used manner adverbs for help

---

[13] *OED2* s.v. Glance 5.
[14] *OED2* s.v. Stare 1.a.
[15] *OED2* s.v. Glare 2.
[16] *OED2* s.v. Peep 1.

158

in describing characters' eye behavior? Examining examples of *looked* using AntConc, the percentages of the collocation of *looked* as a node and *-ly* manner adverbs as its modifier within four words on the right side of it are 0.07 (74/1007) in the HNC and 0.21 (113/520) in the reference corpus, respectively. In this way, Hemingway's descriptions of eye behavior tend to solely communicate the characters' act of looking without minutely conveying their manner.

At the same time, however, a question may arise from this result. How does the author leave us deeply impressed with his characters' eye behavior? Is only the high frequency of basic verbs of visual perception responsible for such an impression? Or, are there other stylistic factors that should be considered as well? The following excerpt may give us a hint:

(23)   'What's the matter, Frances?'
        'Oh, nothing,' she said, 'except that he wants to leave me.'
        'How do you mean?'
        'Oh, he told every one that we were going to be married, and I told my mother and every one, and now he doesn't want to do it.'
        'What's the matter?'
        'He's decided he hasn't lived enough. I knew it would happen when he went to New York.'
        She **looked** up, **very bright-eyed** and trying to talk inconsequentially.
        'I wouldn't marry him if he doesn't want to. Of course I wouldn't. I wouldn't marry him now for anything. But it does seem to me to be a little late now, after we've waited three years, and I've just gotten my divorce.'
        I said nothing.
        'We were going to celebrate so, and instead we've just had scenes. It's so childish. We have dreadful scenes, and he cries and begs me to be reasonable, but he says he just can't do it.'
        'It's rotten luck.'
        'I should say it is rotten luck. I've wasted two years and a half on him now. And I don't know now if any man will ever want to marry me. Two years ago I could have married anybody I wanted, down at Cannes. All the old ones that wanted to marry somebody chic and settle down were crazy about me. Now I don't think I could get anybody.'
        'Sure, you could marry anybody.'

'No, I don't believe it. And I'm fond of him, too. And I'd like to have children. I always thought we'd have children.'

She *looked at* me *very brightly*. 'I never liked children much, but I don't want to think I'll never have them. I always thought I'd have them and then like them.'

'He's got children.'

'Oh, yes. He's got children, and he's got money, and he's got a rich mother, and he's written a book, and nobody will publish my stuff, nobody at all. It isn't bad, either. And I haven't got any money at all. I could have had alimony, but I got the divorce the quickest way.'

She *looked at* me again *very brightly*.

'It isn't right. It's my own fault and it's not, too. I ought to have known better. And when I tell him he just cries and says he can't marry. Why can't he marry? I'd be a good wife. I'm easy to get along with. I leave him alone. It doesn't do any good.'

'It's a rotten shame.'

'Yes, it is a rotten shame. But there's no use talking about it, is there? Come on, let's go back to the café.' (Ch. 6)

In this excerpt, Frances, who is going out with Cohn with the intention of marriage, is explaining her own sentiments to the narrator, Jake, about their breakup, which Cohn has recently brought up. Frances' attempt to act casually with false cheer is articulated by her eye behavior. The author describes the behavior using syntactically succinct and similar sentences in the narrow space of the narrative, collocating *looked* with *bright(ly)* three times. The imbalance of Frances' bright countenance emphasized by the collocational repetition and the heavy content of her consultation serves to highlight her serious situation and complex inner states effectively.

In *The Sun Also Rises*, we find *bright* 15 times in total, including *bright-eyed* in (23). Out of the 15 instances, only three are related to the descriptions of characters, all of which are used for depicting Frances. Likewise, *brightly*, used three times in *The Sun Also Rises*, occurs exclusively for describing Frances. What is more, they all appear recurrently in the same context as (23). The three examples of this are as follows:

160

(24) Now for the first time [Frances] dropped her **bright**, terribly cheerful **manner**. (Ch. 6)

(25) [Frances] turned to me with that terribly **bright smile**. (Ch. 6)

(26) Frances was talking on to [Cohn], **smiling brightly**, looking into his face [. . .] (Ch. 6)

The instances of *bright(ly)* used to depict a character in *The Sun Also Rises* are all confined to the descriptions of Frances. It must be noted that the collocation of 'smile' or 'manner' and *bright(ly)* for her facial expressions[17] in (24), (25), and (26) resonates in the same context with the collocation *looked* and *bright(ly)* for her eye behavior, succeeding in giving us a deep impression of her state of mind.

As briefly mentioned above, repetition has been often pointed out as one of Hemingway's stylistic characteristics.[18] In truth, exactly the same or similar expressions, which often include verbs of visual perception, recurrently appear at short or long intervals in the author's works. Consequently, characters' personalities or states of mind are engraved in us, often with a feeling of tension. In the above section 4.2., we observed the author's repetitive use of Brett's facial expressions containing *eyes*. The following quotations (27)–(31) will make it clear that such a writing style can also be found in examples of her eye behavior:

(27) We drove straight down, turning around the Lion de Belfort that guards the passing Montrouge trams. Brett *looked straight ahead*. (Ch. 4)

(28) Bill was sitting at the table pouring another glass of Fundador. Brett was sitting *looking straight ahead* at nothing. (Ch. 16)

(29) Brett was nervous as I had never seen her before. She kept looking away from me and *looking ahead* at the wall. (Ch. 16)

(30) Trees were dark along the banks. We sat and looked out. Brett *stared straight ahead*. Suddenly she shivered. (Ch. 16)

(31) After a little I felt Brett stiffen beside me, and saw she was *looking straight ahead*. (Ch. 18)

---

[17] It can be easily understood by context that *her bright, terribly cheerful manner* in (24) is mainly describing Frances' facial expression.

[18] See, for example, Bridgman (1966).

As these excerpts suggest, Brett's feeling of apprehension is portrayed in the same way by means of collocating verbs of visual perception (four out of five are the basic one 'look') with the phrase *straight ahead* (except only *ahead* in (29)). In *The Sun Also Rises*, we can find three more examples of this collocation. They are used, however, only for describing the bearing of the matadors. We may say, accordingly, that this collocation is purposefully employed by Hemingway as one almost exclusively for portraying Brett's eye behavior. Similarly, the quotations (32) and (33) come from the same context:

(32) [Brett] was *looking into my eyes* with that way she had of looking that made you wonder whether she really saw out of her own eyes. (Ch. 4)

(33) [Brett] had been *looking into my eyes* all the time. Her eyes had different depths, sometimes they seemed perfectly flat. (Ch. 4)

Such a collocation as 'look into one's eyes' is never seen in any of the descriptions of characters other than Brett in *The Sun Also Rises*. Furthermore, we may note, in passing, that Hemingway's works have only two other instances of a collocation including 'look up into one's eyes.' In this way, the instances of stereotypical collocation used intensively for Brett in (27)–(33) play a key part in producing her bewitching attraction, which is absolutely significant for *The Sun Also Rises*, as well as for betraying her inner states of mind, her apprehension and her fear.

5. Final Remarks
In the first section, I outlined the tendency of words for body language to be employed by several American authors, including Mark Twain, Willa Cather, F. Scott Fitzgerald, with a main focus on Ernest Hemingway. Then, the second section confined itself to a case study of one of Hemingway's novels, *The Sun Also Rises*, so as to inquire into his wording for facial expressions and eye behavior mainly from a collocational viewpoint.

This case study unveiled some stylistic tendencies of the author's use of facial expressions and eye behavior, which are sure to give us clues to better understand his comprehensive style of non-verbal communication.

First, the comparatively low frequency of *eyes* and the selectively high frequency of basic verbs of visual perception, which can be identified generally in the author's short stories, can also be observed in *The Sun Also Rises*.

Second, instances of collocation between *eyes*, *face*, and the verb 'look' as a node and their modifiers are not unique in themselves but conventional and banal to a large extent. However, Hemingway was inclined to use such examples of common collocation recurrently and almost exclusively for particular characters' facial expressions and eye behavior. This stylistic strategy, which is sometimes hardly noticeable, is one of the vital factors for creating the idiosyncratic atmosphere in *The Sun Also Rises*.

Based on the findings of this paper, my future research will be carried out with a much closer reading and analysis of Hemingway's writings in order to reveal how his descriptive use of body language, in particular his depiction of facial expressions and eye behavior, works systematically and structurally in his novels and short stories.

References

Bridgman, Richard. 1966. *The colloquial style in America*. New York: Oxford University Press.

Culpeper, Jonathan. 2001. *Language and characterisation: People in plays and other texts*. London: Routledge.

Eschholz, Paul A. 1973. Mark Twain and the language of gesture. *The Mark Twain Journal* 17, 5–8.

Fischer, Victor. 1983. Foreword. *The Prince and the Pauper*. By Mark Twain. Berkeley: University of California Press.

Gliserman, Martin. 1996. *Psychoanalysis, language, and the body of the text*. Gainesville: University Press of Florida.

Hardy, Donald E. 2007. *The body in Flannery O'Connor's fiction: Computational technique and linguistic voice*. Columbia: The University of South Carolina Press.

Hori, Masahiro. 2004. *Investigating Dickens' style: A collocational analysis.* Basingstoke: Palgrave Macmillan.

Korte, Barbara. 1997. *Body language in literature.* Toronto: University of Toronto Press.

Mahlberg, Michaela. 2013. *Corpus stylistics and Dickens's fiction.* New York: Routledge.

Quirk, Randolph, Sidney Greenbaum, Geoffrey Leech & Jan Svartvik. 1985. *A comprehensive grammar of the English language.* London: Longman.

Takeshita, Hirotoshi. 2015. AntConc o riyoshita heminguwei tanpen sakuhin no tokucho go ni kansuru ichi kosatsu [Stylistic study of keywords in Ernest Hemingway's short stories as taken by AntConc]. *Bulletin* 47, 63–72.

_____. 2016. Denshi kopasu o riyoshita Mark Twain no korokeshon kenkyu: *The Prince and the Pauper* no hyojo byosha ni mirareru shintai goi ni tsuite [Collocational study of Mark Twain's novels made with electric corpora: With special reference to body-part nouns for facial expressions in *The Prince and the Pauper*]. In Masahiro Hori (ed.), *Kopasu to eigo buntai* [*Corpus and English stylistics*], 103–31. Tokyo: Hituzi Syobo.

Index

A

Across the River and into the Trees 135, 149–50, 152, 154

Ancrene Wisse 8, 11, 15–16, 18

AntConc 3, 7, 25, 110, 134, 140, 158

Austen, J. 41–3, 45, 49–52, 54–5, 58, 60–1

B

back formation 124

Bartlett, J. 23

Belinda 43, 47–8

Bible, the 3, 4, 7, 10, 14–15

blush(ing) 41–61

bodily word(s) 110–11, 125

body language 23–4, 41–3, 54, 56–8, 60–1, 63, 70, 72, 83, 85, 89, 109, 112–13, 115, 117, 120–5, 128, 133–4, 137–40, 146, 161–2

body-part noun(s) 111–12, 125, 128, 138, 141–3, 146, 148, 150, 153

Brook, G. L. 116, 125

Bulwer, J. 37

Burney, F. 43, 121

C

Cather, W. 134, 136–7, 141–2, 156, 161

character identification 124

(character's) state(s) of mind 45, 64–6, 82, 88, 95–7, 104, 109, 115, 122, 124, 128, 139–41, 145, 147, 160–1

characterization 51, 55, 85–6, 90, 104, 115–16, 124, 137–8

psychological characterization 115

characters' eyes 63–4, 82–3, 85–6, 88, 90, 95, 104–5

Chaucer, G. 2, 7, 12–14, 16–19

Chirologia 37

Chironomia 37

Clarissa 43–5, 89

Clarke, M. C. 23

collocation(s) 1, 27, 44, 47, 51, 64–7, 82, 86–90, 101, 112–16, 119, 128, 139, 142, 148, 150–5, 158–62

common collocation 1, 139, 162

conventional collocation 51, 139

metaphorical collocation 90

stereotypical collocation 161

unusual (or deviant) collocation 89–90, 101, 116, 128

Connor, S. 86

Cymbeline 25, 29–33

D

David Copperfield 85, 115, 119, 123

Dickens, C.   85–6, 89–91, 95, 104–5, 109–20, 123–6, 128, 137–9
Dickens Corpus   110–13, 116–19, 139
Dickens Lexicon Digital   117
Dictionary of Old English Corpus   3
dramatization   54, 125

E
Edgeworth, M.   43
18th Works Corpus   112, 116–19
Emma   43, 50–1, 55–6, 60–1
Emmeline 43, 46–7
emotional display   124
Eschholz, P.   133–4
Evelina   43, 47, 52, 121
externalisers   121
eye behavior   63–4, 68–83, 85–6, 95–7, 99–101, 104–5, 133–4, 138–40, 145–6, 156–62

F
Fitzgerald, F. S.   134, 136–7, 139, 141–2, 156, 161
facial expression(s)   41, 56, 133–4, 138, 140–2, 146, 148, 150, 152, 155–6, 160–2
Farewell to Arms, A   134, 149–50, 153–4
For Whom the Bell Tolls   135, 149–50, 153, 155
Fowler, R.   96

G
Gaskell, E   63–4, 82–3
Gorman, A. G.   41–2, 50
Gregory, J.   42, 50

H
Hard Times   85–6, 89–90, 96, 105
Hemingway, E.   133–5, 137, 139–43, 145–6, 148–53, 155–8, 160–2

highlighting function   123
Hori, M.   1, 85, 109–10, 138–9
hyperbolic   91

I
Inchbald, E.   43, 46
Innsbruck Corpus of Middle English Prose (ICoMEP)   7
irony   102, 123
ironical attitude   124

K
Karim-Cooper, F.   34–5
keyword(s)   140–1, 145, 156–7
negative keyword(s)   140–2, 145– 6, 156–7
Kobayashi, Y.   121
Korte, B.   41, 43, 54, 63, 68–70, 72, 80, 83, 89, 95, 109, 112, 121, 124–5, 134, 137–8

L
Leavis, F. R.   85–6
lemmatization   109–10
literal contrast   94
Littlemore, J.   34

M
Mahlberg, M.   123, 125, 137, 139
Mansfield Park   50, 52
McMaster, J.   41–3
metonymy   34, 100
Mono, S.   123
Mysteries of Udolpho, The   43

N
Nicholas Nickleby   119–20
19th Works Corpus   110–12, 116–19
Northanger Abbey   50, 55

O
O'Farrell, M.   42

Old Man and the Sea, The 135, 149–50, 154
Oliver Twist 85, 113–5, 119–20
Our Mutual Friend 117, 120

P
Page, N. 109
Pamela 43–5, 86, 88–90
Paris Psalter, the 7, 15
participial adjective(s) 139, 142, 145
Pericles 25, 29, 32, 35–7
periphrasis 101
Piers Plowman 7, 13–14
Pride and Prejudice 42, 50

R
Radcliffe, A. 43, 50
Richardson, S. 42–3, 45–6, 49–50, 61, 86, 88–90

S
Seto, K. 34
Shakespeare, W. 23–7, 29–31, 34–5, 38, 137
Sylvia's Lovers 63–4, 68, 82
Simple Story, A 43, 46–7, 49
Smith, C. 43
Spevack, M. 23
stage direction 34
Stone, H. 91
Sucksmith, H. 91, 102

Sun Also Rises, The 133–4, 140, 146–50, 152–6, 159–62
synonymous adjective(s) 115–16
symbolic 6, 15, 86, 91, 95–6, 104

T
Tale of Two Cities, A 113–14, 116, 120, 125–6
Tempest, The 25, 29, 32, 35–6
temporary emotion 80
To Have and Have Not 135, 149–50, 152–3
Todd, J. 41
Torrents of Spring, The 134, 149–50, 153
transferred epithet(s) 67, 80, 87, 92, 94, 114–16, 126
Troilus and Criseyde 17, 19
Twain, M. 133–41, 143, 145, 161

V
verb(s) of visual perception 82, 139, 145–6, 148, 156–8, 160–2

W
Watanabe, T. 96
Wiltshire, J. 42, 48, 50, 55
Winter's Tale, The 25, 29–30

Y
Yamamoto, T. 117, 124

Studies in the History of the English Language ⑧

A Chronological and Comparative Study of Body Language in English and American Literature

編　者　堀　正広　池田裕子　高口圭轉

発行者　武村哲司

2018 年 10 月 23 日　　第 1 版第 1 刷発行ⓒ

発行所　株式会社　開 拓 社

〒113–0023 東京都文京区向丘 1–5–2
電話 03–5842–8900（代表）
振替 00160–8–39587
http://www.kaitakusha.co.jp

印刷　日之出印刷株式会社　　　　　　ISBN978–4–7589–2268–5 C3382